Leadership M

MW01134581

The evidence is clear – school leaders make a difference to the learning of the pupils they serve. Yet, not all leaders have the same degree of impact. What are the factors that make the difference to student learning? Why are some leaders able to raise student achievement in schools in the most challenging circumstances, whilst other leaders struggle to simply maintain the status quo?

Drawing from international case study research over many years, from the experience of hundreds of school leaders serving widely diverse communities, Linda Kaser and Judy Halbert argue that there are six distinct mindsets that characterize the way successful, learning-oriented leaders operate and make sense of their professional world. These leaders are:

- motivated by intense moral purpose
- knowledgeable about current models of learning
- consistently inquiry-oriented
- able to build trusting relationships
- evidence-informed
- able to move to wise action.

This book outlines an alternative way of thinking about school leadership. It examines research evidence that leaders will find most useful and suggests how they might use this evidence to maximise their learning and the learning of their students. *Leadership Mindsets* has been written specifically for aspiring to newly-appointed school leaders who are determined and motivated to create quality and equality for learners in the schools they serve, through networks of inquiry, learning and support.

Linda Kaser is a co-leader of the Network of Performance Based Schools and a faculty member in Leadership Studies at the University of Victoria and Vancouver Island University, Canada.

Judy Halbert is a co-leader of the Network of Performance Based Schools and a faculty member in Leadership Studies at the University of Victoria and Vancouver Island University, Canada.

Leading School Transformation

Series Editors:

Alma Harris
University of London, UK

Claire Mathews
Head of Leadership programmes, Specialist Schools and Academic Trust

Sue Williamson
Director of Leadership and Innovation, Specialist Schools and Academies Trust

The Leading School Transformation series brings together leading researchers and writers to identify the latest thinking about new and innovative leadership practices that transform schools and school systems. The books have been written with educational professionals in mind, and draw upon the latest international research and evidence to offer new ways of thinking about leadership; provide examples of leadership in practice; and identify concrete ways of transforming leadership for schools and school systems in the future.

Leadership Mindsets
Innovation and learning in the transformation of schools
Linda Kaser and Judy Halbert

Also available in this series:

Raising the Stakes
From improvement to transformation in the reform of schools
Brian J. Caldwell and Jim Spinks

Distributed School Leadership
Developing tomorrow's leaders
Alma Harris

Leadership Mindsets

Innovation and learning in the transformation of schools

Linda Kaser and Judy Halbert

Routledge
Taylor & Francis Group
LONDON AND NEW YORK

iNet
International Networking for
Educational Transformation

Specialist Schools
and Academies Trust
EXCELLENCE AND DIVERSITY

First published 2009
by Routledge
2 Park Square, Milton Park, Abingdon, Oxon OX14 4RN, UK

Simultaneously published in the USA and Canada
by Routledge
270 Madison Ave, New York, NY 10016

Reprinted 2009, 2010

Routledge is an imprint of the Taylor & Francis Group, an informa business

© 2009 Linda Kaser and Judy Halbert

Typeset in Garamond3 by
RefineCatch Limited, Bungay, Suffolk
Printed and bound in Great Britain by
TJ International Ltd, Padstow, Cornwall

British Library Cataloguing in Publication Data
A catalogue record for this book is available from the British Library

Library of Congress Cataloging-in-Publication Data
Kaser, Linda.
   Leadership mindsets : innovation and learning in the transformation
   of schools / Linda Kaser and Judy Halbert.
      p. cm. – (Leading school transformation)
   Includes bibliographical references and index.
   1. Educational leadership.   2. Educational innovations.   3. School
   management and organization.   I. Halbert, Judy, 1949-   II. Title.
LB2805.K367 2009
371.2—dc22
                                                          2008034285

ISBN10: 0–415–47693–3 (hbk)
ISBN10: 0–415–47694–1 (pbk)
ISBN10: 0–203–88115–X (ebk)

ISBN13: 978–0–415–47693–5 (hbk)
ISBN13: 978–0–415–47694–2 (pbk)
ISBN13: 978–0–203–88115–6 (ebk)

For Frances, Kate and Sam

Contents

Illustrations

Acknowledgements

The book has been enriched and informed by the leadership stories, practices, insights and commitments of the members of the Network of Performance Based Schools, of the new school leaders in the Certificate of School Management and Leadership program at the University of Victoria and by the rural and urban participants in the New Leaders professional development program of the BC Educational Leadership Council. We sincerely thank each of these educators for their enthusiasm for learning and for their passion for making a positive impact on the lives of all learners.

We also appreciate the intellectual friendship of our colleagues in the International Congress of School Effectiveness and Improvement as their thinking has influenced us and their interest has motivated us.

The series editor, Alma Harris, has provided invaluable encouragement and support for our leadership thinking.

Series foreword
Leading school transformation

It is now widely accepted that transforming schools is at the heart of system-wide transformation. In order to raise the educational bar while closing the performance gap there has to be continual and relentless attention to improving teaching and learning in our schools. This is unlikely to be achieved unless school leaders are committed to school reform and renewal. This requires leaders who understand the importance of working at both the school and the system level. It also requires leaders who are able to invest in the leadership of others and to share leadership practice widely and deeply.

The 'Specialist Schools and Academies Trust' (SSAT) seeks to give more young people access to a good education by building networks, sharing practice and supporting schools. The Trust's way of working is based on the principle 'by schools for schools' and it is at the heart of a growing network of over 4,500 schools including primary, secondary, special schools and academies in England, as well as schools elsewhere in the UK and internationally. As one of the largest school networks of its kind, it is working with school leaders to explore and trial next practice.

The international arm of the Trust is iNet – 'International Networking for Educational Transformation'. iNet exists to create networks of schools in countries around the world that can innovate and transform schools and school systems. Its prime aim is to secure systematic and sustained change that has a positive impact on young people's achievement. There are currently school networks in Australia, China, Chile, Mauritius, New Zealand, Northern Ireland, South Africa, Sweden, USA (Georgia and Boston) and Wales. iNet schools, institutions and individuals have the opportunity to share innovation and work collaboratively.

I am delighted that SSAT and iNet will be working with Routledge over the next few years to establish the 'Leading School Transformation' series. This is an important series because it will bring together the foremost thinkers and writers in the field of leadership and educational transformation. This is exemplified by the inaugural book by Brian Caldwell and Jim Spinks – *Resourcing Schools: From improvement to transformation in the reform of schools.* It is thought-provoking, challenging and very timely. It asks us to think differently about school development, leadership and system reform. It advocates raising the stakes and moving from satisfaction with school improvement to accepting the challenge to transform young people's learning and achievement.

I look forward to reading the other books in the SSAT/iNet series and know that schools all over the world will find this series a source of challenge and inspiration.

Elizabeth Reid
Chief Executive of the Specialist Schools and Academies Trust

Foreword

Books on leadership continue to fill bookshelves across the world. In this 'golden age' of leadership it is rare to find a book that is more concerned with learning than leadership styles, approaches or models. In *Leadership Mindsets* Linda Kaser and Judy Halbert have clearly and convincingly made the case that leadership is fundamentally about learning and essentially for learning.

Drawing upon their extensive experience as teachers, principals, presenters and researchers, the book is grounded in the realities of schools and schooling. It is evident that these two authors have 'walked the talk'. The practical examples and illustrations shared throughout the book offer important lenses on the world of teachers and teaching and provide insightful commentary and observation.

But do not be mistaken, this is not a 'how to do book' or 'tips for teachers'. The book is punctuated with references to the latest research and incorporates some of the most recent evidence about leadership and learning. Kaser and Halbert combine intellectual rigour with practical illustration and application. Their blend of theory and practice is presented with finesse and authenticity.

The book is refreshing because it challenges leaders to think deeply about learning and learners. Changing mindsets and changing practice is at the heart of this book. It argues that what is missing in many leadership preparation and professional development programs, and until recently in much of the school leadership theory and research literature, is the direct connection between school leadership and improvements in student learning. This is certainly true, as the forces of accountability have ironically distracted leaders from what matters most, learning and teaching.

This book provides both established and new leaders with mindsets that focus directly upon learning. The book explores the relationship between leadership and school change, transformation and improvement. No blueprint is provided but the combination of intense moral purpose, trust, inquiry and learning orientated design offer powerful levers for change. Kaser and Halbert want schools to move from a sorting system to a learning system. They argue that this will require adaptive expertise and innovative approaches. It will also require leaders who are guided by internal accountability and professional judgement and not driven by external weighing, measuring and grading. Schools that improve and sustain improvement are guided by strong internal accountability processes that focus exclusively on student learning.

In the current educational landscape gains in school and student performance can be short lived. The political imperative to increase test scores often outweighs the moral, social and educational purpose of schooling. The net result is that successive cohorts of young people have been sorted by the education system rather than nurtured by it.

It is time for schools to reclaim the lost territory of learning and for school leaders to refocus their considerable expertise and energy upon engaging and supporting the learning of all students, in all settings and from all backgrounds. To secure equity and quality in education, as Kaser and Halbert so ably argue, will require changing mindsets and refocusing on core educational values. This message has never been so timely, or so important.

Alma Harris (Series Editor)

Introduction

This book has been written to encourage new and experienced school leaders to consider six leadership mindsets that we believe are fundamental to school and system transformation. Readers will be able to learn from the experiences of other formal and informal school leaders who are focused passionately on learning and who are working hard to transform their schools. We hope that hearing their voices and their stories will bring the concepts to life for you.

In addition to our own studies of leadership theories and practice-based research, we have both been principals and vice principals in a range of settings – in schools in affluent and poor communities, ranging in size from 170 to 1900 students, and in levels from primary through senior secondary. We know from these experiences that school leadership is action-oriented and fast paced. Having the time to examine current research to inform leadership practice is a luxury principals cannot routinely afford, yet our learners need our practice to be influenced by the best of current knowledge and thinking.

Leadership is easy to talk about, reasonably easy to write about and challenging to do well in practice. In schools across the world there are principals, head teachers, teachers, department leaders, curriculum coordinators, and team leaders all providing leadership through their formal or informal roles. If you are new to a formal leadership role, this book is designed to assist you in connecting research and practice by using the mindsets to shift your schools to places of deep, engaged and lifelong learning. If you are an experienced leader, we hope that you can see some of your experiences reflected in the leaders we profile and that you can use the mindsets to deepen and strengthen the learning orientation in your school. If you are a teacher leader interested in making an even stronger contribution to the learning of your colleagues and young people, we believe the mindsets can provide a useful framework for your thinking.

In our own work we have learned a great deal from the perspectives of distributed, ethical, instructional, strategic, sustainable and transformational theories of leadership. We have also read with interest and discussed and thought about most of the other 'adjectival' forms – from authoritarian, bad, breakthrough, and charismatic, through to supervisory, toxic, turnaround and questioning leadership. Yet our own school leadership experiences, combined with our case studies of schools and their leaders over the past ten years, have led us to conclude that school leaders, who are leading in a complex period of technological, environmental, social, economic and political change, need to focus their leadership learning and thinking in six critical areas. We describe these areas as mindsets to capture the notion that they are broad cognitive-emotional capacities rather than narrow forms of behavioral competencies. The concepts underlying the mindsets have been informed by current research and have practical uses. The new school leaders with whom we work have found the mindset conceptualization to be intellectually helpful and pragmatically useful in their school transformation work.

As school leadership can be a lonely job, we hope that you have a reflective learning partner with whom you can read this book and discuss your own leadership experiences. Jan Robertson's (2005, 2008) work on coaching leadership has had an influence internationally on school leadership practice. Her studies have emphasized the importance of engaging reflectively with a learning partner. She has taken the idea of 'reflection in action' (Schön, 1983) and developed practical strategies to make the reflective model work for new leaders. We hope that the combined voices of real leaders working in real schools, along with the research evidence behind the mindsets, will provide you with a useful way of thinking and talking about your own context with a learning partner. This book is also intended for these leadership learning partners.

We agree with Andy Hargreaves and Dean Fink (2006) who have argued, 'Change in education is easy to propose, hard to implement, and extraordinarily difficult to sustain' (p. 1). Our own experience indicates that constructive changes in school practices are both necessary and possible. We also believe that improvements and transformations can be sustained over time if they are embedded in strong cultures of deep learning and supported by intelligent leadership.

We have found that persistent work on combining intense purpose, a focus on deep learning, informed evidence-seeking, genuine inquiry-mindedness, and thoughtfully designed professional learning in the context of respectful and trusting relationships, benefits the school as a whole and the young people in it. The application of the leadership mindsets are good for the leader, the school, and most importantly, for the learners – especially those who have traditionally been under-served and less than successful.

Over the past 10 years we have worked with hundreds of school leaders in a variety of settings. We have found that the mindsets provide a framework for leaders to use in considering their own leadership actions and for thinking about how to move their schools forward as learning systems. Leaders working within the structure of the mindsets are better able to sustain their focus on deep learning improvement and are less likely to be buffeted by changes in policy direction or to fall into the trap of hyperactively responding to the many competing demands for their time and attention. Schools characterized by intense moral purpose – where trusting relationships are nurtured and inquiry-mindedness is a way of life, where learning is vibrant and engaging for young people and adults – are exciting and rewarding places in which to learn and to work. In these schools, learners do not fall through the cracks, fade out, drop out or drift along. We are inspired by the leaders in schools who are genuinely personalizing learning, finding new and powerful ways to support all learners and who are engaging families as valued partners. We know the difference that school leaders can make from our own experience, from our case study research and from international studies.

All the mindsets are important and they are all linked. In the busy world of schools, it would be an illusion for school leaders to think, 'I will build trust first and then I will think about learning and inquiry.' A staff member who expresses confusion, irritation, curiosity or interest provides the opportunity for the leader to demonstrate both trustworthiness and inquiry-mindedness – on the spot. A leader approached by a parent who is concerned about the way her child is being treated by her teacher will draw on the mindsets of evidence, trust, inquiry and intense moral purpose. A district request that schools submit a technology improvement plan in response to a new government announcement requires a leader to draw on the mindsets of evidence, trust, inquiry and learning-oriented design. We have tried, through the mindsets, to connect the world of research and the reality of leadership action for you. We hope the questions provided at the end of each chapter will provide a starting point for your personal reflections and discussion with a leadership partner.

Overview of the leadership mindsets

Chapter 1 Moving from sorting to learning – new mindsets required

As Alma Harris has noted, 'the education terrain is rapidly shifting and the existing structures and boundaries of schooling are fast eroding' (2008, p. 19). Chapter 1 provides a rationale as to why new leadership mindsets are required in the new terrain of education as schools make the shift from sorting to deep learning for all. The thinking of Carol Dweck (2006), Howard Gardner (2007) and Henry Mintzberg (2004) has helped to shape our conceptualization of mindsets. The ideas of Daniel Schwartz, John Bransford and David Sears (2005) reinforce the importance of adaptive expertise in the work of school transformation. Innovation and transformation are terms easily bandied about by theoreticians and policy-makers. What do they really mean for school principals caught up in the daily challenges of deepening the learning culture in their schools, often in a constrained resource environment?

Chapter 2 Intense moral purpose

Leadership in schools is about making a difference in the lives of learners – each learner and all learners. Intense moral purpose is connected with passionate and persistent intensity and as Christopher Day and Ken Leithwood (2007) recently observed: 'Passion is not a luxury, a frill or a quality possessed by just a few principals. It is essential to sustaining successful leadership' (p. 176). It has also been argued that the moral imperative of school leaders must be both broader within the school and wider outside the school than it has been in the past (Fullan 2003). The moral purpose mindset asks you, as a school leader, to explore what the notions of quality and equity mean, and to consider the implications of developing new forms of quality. You will think about the importance of school identity and sustainability as they connected with moral purpose. As you meet Alison, a new principal in a remote community serving highly vulnerable learners and Karim, a principal in an urban high school serving many refugee families, we invite you to think carefully about the learners you serve.

Chapter 3 Trust – relationships first

In Chapter 3 you will explore findings from a longitudinal study, *Trust in Schools* (Bryk and Schneider 2003), which provides evidence that schools with low levels of relational trust have only a one-in-seven chance of demonstrating improved academic learning. You will think about the connection between trust and transformation. From her study of five secondary schools, Karen Seashore Louis (2007) showed that as a school leader you need to understand 'trust as the bridge that reform must be carried over, but rather than being solid, that bridge is built on changing emotions' (p. 20). Without a strong focus on developing or strengthening trusting relationships the bitter reality is that little change will occur – and the absence of trust works to the detriment of learners who need newer pedagogies to thrive.

You will follow Chris as he strives to build trust in a secondary school plagued by poor relationships. You will examine four key components of trust: respect, personal regard, integrity and competence in core responsibilities. You will think about the way you are establishing trust and personal regard through your day-to-day interactions. You will consider the importance of respect in the way you approach conflict and respond to diverse cultures and points of view. You will think about the relationship between trust and competence in the core responsibilities inherent in organizing and managing a school. Finally, you will consider the way you are building trust to create a bridge to deep learning reform.

Chapter 4 Inquiry – questions before directions

A spirit of inquiry-mindedness and a variety of forms of inquiry can assist new leaders in realizing their moral purpose of improved learning for all. Leaders with an inquiry mindset reflect Lieberman and Miller's (2004) perspective that:

> An inquiry stance is far different from a solution stance. It requires that one ask questions of one's practice rather than look for answers. It places contextual data collection and analysis

rather than generalized solutions at the center of improvement efforts.

(p. 41)

Here you will meet Cathy, a new primary principal with an inquiry habit of mind. You will follow her efforts to apply four forms of inquiry – narrative, appreciative, critical, and reflective – in her work to deepen the learning culture of her school. You will think about your own approach to making sense of the problems in your school. To what extent are you applying different forms of inquiry? How are you developing your own sense of inquiry? How are you encouraging a spirit of inquiry among your colleagues?

Chapter 5 Learning for deeper understanding

Chapter 5 introduces and overviews some contemporary understandings of learning. If meaningful professional development and productive learning-focused supervisory practices are to be a reality, leaders must be able to hold thoughtful conversations about learning with every teacher. Leaders must know how to serve as 'intellectual companions' to educators at varying stages in their careers and at various developmental levels. Leaders who are familiar with and can apply thinking from a model or framework for learning are better equipped to lead schools in which deep learning – for both young people and adults – is a way of life.

Here we follow the story of Geoff, a secondary school principal with a strong commitment to lifelong learning. You will see him develop an understanding of major theoretical approaches to learning, and knowledge of a set of well developed learning principles. You will also explore a number of models or frameworks of learning that consciously draw on post-Vygotsky (1978) understandings. You will consider how developing knowledge of self-regulated, imaginative, lifelong, and effort-based learning will help you lead a school where the learning program reflects the importance of critical thinking and adaptive expertise.

Chapter 6 Evidence-seeking in action

In this chapter you will think about the role of evidence in shifting from a sorting to a learning system. In many parts of the world schools have been described as being data-rich and information-poor.

Leaders need to carefully consider what they say about what 'counts' in their school. An evidence-informed mindset requires understanding the role of formative assessment practices, engagement and metacognition in learning.

What types of information truly provide evidence of deep learning? How is knowledge of assessment *for* and *as* learning being applied to support deeper learning? You will meet Donna, a new secondary vice principal who turned her concern about the lack of success of a group of Year 9 learners into thoughtful, team-oriented action. You will explore the forms of evidence she found compelling and her leadership approach in using this evidence to mobilize staff action.

Chapter 7 Learning-oriented design

The mindsets of intense moral purpose, trust, learning, evidence and inquiry are collectively made apparent through the actions that leaders take to design and support opportunities for adult learning. This is where leadership thinking hits the learning action road.

One of the key responsibilities of school leaders is to create and sustain opportunities for adult learning that lead to improved learning for young people. The notion of design in this chapter reflects the sophistication and complexity required to create appropriate conditions, structures and rhythms for adult learning.

We draw on research and practice evidence about distributed leadership, teacher professional learning, and learning communities of practice to think about the ways in which leaders design adult learning. We will follow the specific ways that Chris, Karim, Donna, Geoff, Alison, and Cathy are organizing for adult learning in their schools.

Chapter 8 Connecting mindsets – networked leadership

Thankfully, the days of the heroic solitary leader 'heading' the school are almost gone. Not only do leaders with the mindsets described in this book naturally and effectively move to a more distributed form of leadership, they also connect with other leaders through networks of inquiry and challenging friendship. In this final chapter, we will explore ways in which school leaders helping their schools shift from sorting to learning are benefiting from connections with other schools and other leaders. You will think about the importance of challenging friendships and reflective learning partnerships in your own setting. And we will examine the power of full engagement and the notion of school leadership as 'good work' as described in the book *Good Work, When Excellence and Ethics Meet* (Gardner et al., 2001).

Chapter 1

Moving from sorting to learning – new mindsets required

The education terrain is rapidly shifting and the existing struc-tures and boundaries of schooling are fast eroding. Education is being revolutionized through the Internet, Google, outsourcing and 24/7 demands and expectations. Those organizations des-tined to be 'great' in the rapidly transforming world will be those adept at generating new leadership capacity to meet the changing demands of global schooling.

Alma Harris (2008, p. 19)
Distributed Leadership: Developing Leaders for Tomorrow

We need leaders to create transformed schools using a new growth mindset: The passion for stretching yourself and stick-ing to it, even (or especially) when it's not going well, is the hallmark of the growth mindset. This is the mindset that allows people to thrive during some of the most challenging times in their lives. This *growth mindset* is based on the belief that your basic qualities are things you can cultivate through your efforts. Although people may differ in every which way – in their initial talents and aptitudes, interests, or temperaments – everyone can change and grow through application and experience.

Carol Dweck (2006: pp. 6–7)
Mindset: The New Psychology of Success

Frances Stone understands that school leadership is about making a difference in the lives of learners. Whenever she has doubts about the meaning of her work, she thinks about Justin, Madeline, Anna and Matt. These children are four of six siblings who live with their father in a small northern community. The town has been hit by serious economic downturns. The factory has closed, unemployment is high and positive future prospects for anyone with less than a good secondary education are remote. There was a time not so long ago when a teacher, principal or head teacher at their school might have looked at these children and described them as having 'little hope' and, although perhaps somewhat embarrassed to do so, other educators would have nodded in agreement.

Fortunately these young people attend a school where the teachers and the leaders have a growth mindset, not a fixed mindset, where the staff passionately believes that they can collectively change the life chances of all their learners for the better. Frances and her staff are dedicated to making sure that each of them has a chance for a full rich life – no matter what it takes. Justin, age eight, has dreams of becoming a writer. A university mentor is helping him to believe in his own storytelling gifts and he recently won a young writers' contest. Two years ago, Madeline, age nine, was a struggling reader. Now she is helping younger readers in her role as a reading coach and is further developing her strong social skills as a peer helper. Anna, 12, is working as a volunteer in the school library and is highly regarded by the staff and students for her service orientation and organizational skills. She provides Internet research assistance for adults in the community and she is considering secondary programme choices in languages and international studies. She is studying advanced mathematics on-line through an innovative distance-learning programme connecting talented teachers and learners.

Matt, 17, is involved in an electronic arts apprenticeship programme in a partnership between his high school and the local college. He is also a volunteer emergency responder in his community as part of his service learning work. Only a year ago, Matt was in danger of becoming a 'fade out' in his school. The teachers and his principal refused to give up on him and he responded to their persistent caring. Now he is on his way to a productive future.

These young people are learning and thriving and their school is providing them with the hand-up they need and deserve.

These four young people live in a very different world than their grandparents and parents. Their schooling needs are also very different. The skills their families needed in order to find factory employment and run households are not nearly enough for these four learners who need to thrive in a world of technological complexity and global connectivity. The demands of contemporary society require that educators rethink many aspects of the school experience, including the roles of informal and formal leaders and the way school leadership generally is conceptualized.

We agree with the arguments proposed by a number of thinkers that the move from an industrial to a knowledge society demands a shift in key assumptions about learning, schooling and leadership. Robert Starratt (2004), for example, contends that the industrial model of the last century developed educational practices that fragmented and trivialized learning and separated school activities from the life worlds of students. Particularly in secondary schools, the truncated class periods, the lack of connection across curricular areas, the absence of ongoing adult-learner relationships and the emphasis on coverage and testing seem increasingly out of step with the interests and needs of young people.

School leaders know that their responsibility for shaping learning for young people is taking place in a rapidly changing economic, social and technological climate. Manuel Castells (2004) describes the impact of these changes:

> Globalization and informationalization, enacted by networks of wealth, technology and power, are transforming our world. They are enhancing our productive capacity, cultural creativity and communication potential. At the same time, they are disenfranchising societies. As institutions of state and organizations of civil society are based on culture, history and geography, the sudden acceleration of the historical tempo and the abstraction of power in a web of computers, are disintegrating existing mechanisms of social control and political representation . . . people all over the world resent the loss of control over their lives, over their environment, their countries and, ultimately over the fate of the Earth (p. 72).

Learners in today's schools live in this new knowledge world and have access to information, ideas and social connections unimaginable a few years ago. Teachers are wondering how to shift their pedagogy so that today's learners are more engaged in their learning. Experienced, new and potential leaders are wondering about the extent of the educational changes that are required – in curriculum, in organizational structures, in adult staff development and in learning strategies. Does everything need to change, as some argue, or will the community nature of school continue to be an important and ongoing part of the evolution of society? Is it true that all schooling will be exclusively delivered by technology with access to information, teachers and assessments available any time and anywhere? Will schools become quaint artifacts of a by-gone era?

In this chapter you will consider the changes in key assumptions about the purpose of schools as systems shift away from sorting to a stronger focus on learning. The deeper and more ongoing forms of learning required by the knowledge society have significant impli-cations for school leaders. We believe unequivocally that quality learning for every learner in a more personalized and responsive system is at the core of today's school mission. We argue that a different way of conceptualizing the work of school leaders, through the application of a new combination of mindsets, is required to meet this transformative challenge.

Despite globalization and technological advancements, most young people like Madeline, Justin, Anna and Matt currently attend schools of one type or another for at least part of their day. In schools worldwide, the industrial model of schooling is, sadly, still very apparent. In the industrial model, one of the expected functions of the school system was to sort and rank students, mainly in relation to access to post secondary opportunities. In sorting schools, teach-ing was understood and indeed rewarded, as covering the formal curriculum and providing opportunities for students to learn. Formal school leaders including principals and head teachers were expected to manage and organize the administrative structures of the school; they could leave the responsibility for teaching to the staff.

The days of learners leaving school with marginal skills and minimal knowledge and being able to participate fully in society are behind us. Simply providing the opportunity for learning is not enough. Comments such as, 'I've done my best to teach them; it's not my problem if they didn't learn' must no longer be heard. As educators it is not only our problem, it is our professional responsi-bility. In the knowledge society, learning – not sorting – is the key mandate of schools as young people now need and are expected to learn during their school years and throughout their lifetimes. This powerful new expectation for schools and systems requires new conceptions of leadership.

In Table 1.1, we identify four major shifts that are necessary in moving from a sorting system to a learning system. The implications

Table 1.1 Shifting from sorting to learning – implications for systems and learners

Systems Shifting	
From Sorting	*To Learning*
A focus on instruction and teaching	A focus on deeper forms of learning
Summative assessment for grading and reporting	Formative assessment to provide descriptive coaching feedback and learner self-regulation
Teaching in isolation	Teaching teams working as learning communities
External centralized pressure	Local internalized commitment, capacity building and responsibility

of these shifts will be considered further in this book as we explore the leadership mindsets.

Making the move from a sorting to a learning system involves all educators at all levels shifting from a fixed to a growth mindset. This means that all educators will act in ways that demonstrate their conviction that virtually all young people can learn and achieve at high levels. Jurisdictions around the world are taking very seriously the imperative of increasing high school completion rates as a minimum requirement for accessing a productive place in the knowledge society. This requires a different way of thinking, new forms of teamwork, focused effort, continuous learning and passionate commitment. Shifting mindsets is neither easy nor trivial work. It reflects a profound and significant set of changes. Carol Dweck (2006), a leading researcher in the area of developmental psychology, describes mindset change in this way:

> Mindset change is not about picking up a few pointers here and there. It's about seeing things in a new way. When people – couples, coaches and athletes, managers and workers, parents and children, teachers and students – change to a growth mindset, they change from a *judge-and-be-judged* framework to a

learn-and-help-learn framework. Their commitment is to growth and growth takes plenty of time, effort and mutual support.

(p. 238)

The sorting system inherent in the industrial paradigm of schooling reflects the fixed mindset with its emphasis on grading and judging. Learning systems require teachers and leaders with growth mindsets in which learning and helping others learn are lifelong pursuits. Other major thinkers agree that our changing world requires new thinking about leadership. Howard Gardner (2007), for example, describes a set of intellectual approaches or leadership minds that he argues are important for contemporary leadership in every field and discipline. Gardner believes that the deeply interconnected world in which we now live requires new capacities that will help leaders be 'better equipped to deal with what is expected, as well as what cannot be anticipated: without these minds, a person will be at the mercy of forces that he or she can't understand, let alone control' (p. 2).

He describes the five required capacities as 'minds'. The disciplined mind has mastered a way of thinking required of the profession. The synthesizing mind can take information from various sources and connect information in ways that make sense for others. The creating mind engages in new and fresh ways of thinking and considers unfamiliar questions. The respectful mind enjoys and learns to work productively with a variety of other people of dramatically different backgrounds and the ethical mind considers how citizens can work together for the greater good rather than just personal self-interest. Gardner (2007) concludes that these five ways of thinking are critical and that they need to work synergistically if we are to successfully meet our contemporary local and global challenges.

Another noted strategic thinker has also been considering mindset changes connected to management practice and management education. Henry Mintzberg (2004) argues that development programmes for business managers have over-emphasized either the science of managing resulting in technocratic calculation or the artistic approach resulting in an 'heroic' style. Mintzberg's studies convinced him of the importance of an engaging and balanced style and he has since worked internationally with other management educators to create a new programme designed around five mindsets. In the reflective mindset, managers learn to reflect on their own experiences and learn how to become more critically discerning. The analytical mindset emphasizes coming up with an insightful way of framing business challenges. The worldly mindset is about managing context and involves the realization that, even in a deeply interconnected world, that the 'globe is made up of all kinds of worlds' (p. 304). The worldly mindset implies that managers must become more sophisticated, appreciative and practical in working with unfamiliar people and settings. The collaborative mindset involves managing relationships and the Japanese style of leading in the background is valued and explored. The final mindset is about action and managing change and Mintzberg and his colleagues believe that 'the world needs managers who change others by first changing themselves' (p. 310).

The work of Dweck (2006), Gardner (2007) and Mintzberg (2004) has influenced aspects of our thinking about the mindsets for new school leaders. We believe that Dweck's perspective about a growth mindset is important for every educator and especially for leaders as they work to shift their schools in the direction of deep learning and away from an overemphasis on coverage and testing. We have seen the mindsets that Gardner and Mintzberg describe in action in some of the leaders we have observed. The six mindsets we describe in this book have been most directly shaped, however, by our studies of hundreds of new and experienced school leaders in a wide range of schools and communities over the last decade. The most successful of these leaders have been able to transform their schools into centres of deep and ongoing learning.

We recognize that we are thinking about new forms of leadership in a context where school and system transformation is increasingly on the minds of politicians, researchers, theorists, educators, parents and the learners themselves. A useful definition of the transformation required to shift schools and systems from sorting to learning has been proposed: 'We define transformation as significant, systematic and sustained change that secures success for all students in all settings, especially under challenging circumstances, thus contributing to the well being of each and every student and of society' (Caldwell and Spinks 2008, p. 4). Transformation of this significance, demanded by the needs of young learners, poses new and exciting challenges for school leaders. Old solutions to old problems will not work. New mindsets and new forms of expertise are required.

Adaptive expertise required

School leadership would be relatively safe and simple if leaders were only faced with problems for which there were already proven solutions. Heifitz and Linsky (2002) make an important distinction between technical problems for which leaders already have the necessary know-how and procedures and adaptive challenges that cannot be solved by someone who provides answers from above. They call these new problems adaptive challenges because they require experiments, new discoveries and adjustments from numerous places in the organization or community. They suggest, 'without learning new ways – changing attitudes, values and behaviours, people cannot make the adaptive leap necessary to thrive in the new environment' (p. 14).

From their research on learning, Daniel Schwartz, John Bransford and David Sears (2005) have been exploring how to make the development of adaptive expertise a way of life for leaders. They make a case for the importance of both innovation and efficiency in developing adaptive expertise. They argue that efficiency-oriented practice can be understood as 'problem-elimination rather than in-depth, sustained problem solving' (p. 26). They go on to suggest that 'individuals who are optimally adaptive have the cognitive power to rearrange their environments and their thinking as they encounter new problems and novel information' (p. 27).

From their perspective, leaders do need to acquire the kinds of well-organized, fluently accessible sets of skills and knowledge that are represented by efficiency. For school leaders, ensuring that the timetable reflects the best possible use of available personnel, that the budget is balanced and that communication with families is clear and effective are organizational skills reflecting efficiency. Leaders also need an innovative approach that requires a movement away from what is momentarily most efficient for the individual or for the organization. Schwartz, Bransford and Sears (2005) suggest that innovation is often preceded by a sense of disequilibrium that signals that certain processes or ways of thinking, or previously learned routines, are not quite working properly. School leaders determined to make the shift from a sorting to a learning system recognize that the old ways of thinking about school are not working for many learners and they understand that adaptive expertise is needed to develop new solutions to the challenges of increasing both quality and equity.

School leaders also understand that they will have to work through a stage of discomfort and imbalance to make the shift from an emphasis on teaching to a focus on deep learning and to shift from learning for some to learning for all. We have observed that the thinking embedded in the mindsets can assist leaders in developing the kind of adaptive expertise they need to address new problems and develop transformative solutions. Schwartz (2005) and his colleagues describe an optimal adaptability corridor that exists between the dimensions of efficiency and innovation. We would argue that school leaders who embody the mindsets 'live' in this corridor. They understand the need for efficiency and display organizational competence and, at the same time, they are passionately focused on developing innovative practices that will better serve the needs of their learners.

Innovation for system transformation

If we accept Brian Caldwell's (2008) definition of transformation as one of significant, systematic and sustained change aimed at the success of all learners, then we must consider what forms of innovation will help us realize this transformation. We think it is important for school leaders to critically examine the various approaches to change being advocated and to determine what forms of innovation will be most likely to get them to their learning system destination effectively – and with the fewest casualties.

We have been in discussions where policy makers and theoreticians argue for 'blowing up' the old and replacing the industrial model structures as quickly as possible. They want a system that is much more individualized and personalized. With a strong emphasis on choice, technology and technological solutions, their new system is focused on the learner being able to obtain individualized instruction, coaching and virtual tutoring. Personalized learning in this new model is available any time and anywhere for any form of learning needed or desired.

Reflecting the demand for greater personalization and system transformation, David Hargreaves (2003, 2006, 2007) suggests changes in school practices including:

• moving from single to multiple schools and institutions;
• merging age and phase levels so that transitions are more self-paced and seamless;

- creating flexible age groupings where learners of a variety of ages work together rather than in grades;
- constructing a curriculum based on competence and project-based, transdisciplinary approaches;
- combining academic and emotional support through the use of vertical tutoring;
- creating smaller, more intimate groupings within large secondary schools;
- developing learners actively as mentors and coaches for other learners;
- distributing leadership more widely with the adults in the school;
- expanding and systematically developing broader forms of student leadership;
- changing to school-led and school-located initial teacher education and ongoing professional learning – led by educators using peer-to-peer learning and networks with a focus on learning improvement from a whole school perspective.

In the schools we have studied that are moving closer to becoming learning systems, many of these strategies are being used, learning is deepening and learners are benefiting. In addition to changes within schools, there are policy thinkers who are suggesting that leaders focus on working more broadly across schools, levels and community agencies. Valerie Hannon (2007) in her work with the Innovation Unit in England urges policy developers and school leaders to pay much more attention to matters of system leadership where school leaders work collaboratively across schools and with agencies. She notes that in England the context for school leadership is changing fast:

> Head teachers today are already taking on the responsibility of leading more than one school; they are co-leading in partnerships and federations; they are leading schools in close collaboration with other agencies, or are providing a range of services themselves, giving children access to much more than education – healthcare for example and other services. Most radically, perhaps, we are beginning to glimpse a future in which the whole idea of 'school' is re-imagined. School leaders are already guiding education beyond school walls, as ICT opens up new possibilities for schooling that needs no 'school'.
>
> (p. 17)

In our own policy development experience we have been in discussions with those who assume as their starting point the ongoing importance of community and personal connections. In British Columbia, for example, literacy advocates are working together across institutions to develop a greater sense of community, stronger coherence and new forms of teamwork. They see schools as central to this work. Advocates such as these see improving the school system in much the same way as the arts community views building on the classical forms of music, art, dance, drama, and opera. Leaders in many arts communities support making art forms accessible to everyone, improving each of the forms using all of what is known and ensuring that changes are made creatively and respectfully. This view of innovation is similar to the studies of positive deviance[1] from the community health field where small yet profoundly important changes make a big difference over time.

Leaders drawn to this perspective are more likely to emphasize learning-oriented classrooms and emotionally supportive school communities. As school and system leaders ourselves, we are chiefly interested in seeing that wise practices are used systemically and that knowledge from both practice and research are connected and put to work immediately for the purposes of deep learning and social justice. We take as a given that some form of community 'school' as a social learning centre will continue to play an important role in building democratic and inclusive societies. Our focus is on ensuring that every aspect of the learning programme, including the learning and teaching strategies selected, reflects the best of current knowledge and practice about learning.

Conclusion

Matt, Anna, Justin and Madeline are in our classrooms today and they, and all other young people, need and deserve to be part of a learning system that will help them learn for a lifetime. We argue that systemically and persistently applying current knowledge about learning, assessment, motivation, inquiry and teacher professional learning – in every classroom and in every school – is in itself a powerful form of innovation. In our exploration of systems around the world we have found very few where there is a systematic focus on comprehensively using the current knowledge base about learning and teaching. Systems that do so are unusual. What is more usual are small islands of knowledge application with bright lights of innovation surrounded by seas of 'sorting business as usual'.

We agree with Michael Fullan (2006, p. 44), who argues that schools and systems improve when we do what we know works from both research literature and practice and when we do this with greater intensity. We have experienced the positive impact on learning when a school takes a deliberate and sustained approach to improving learning and teaching practices. We have also witnessed the cynicism that occurs when teachers feel burdened by initiative overload and when the focus for improvement efforts or professional learning varies according to the interests of whoever is making the decisions.

As Canadian educators, we are drawn to the forms of change that reflect the best aspects of the credit union movement – a movement that has helped create communities that are generally responsive, socially aware, environmentally active, organizationally sound and financially reliable. We appreciate the credit union blend of strong social connections with more personalized responses embedded in community. We will always seek out those innovations or proposed reforms that are designed to increase both equity and quality because we believe that contemporary school leaders need to work on both goals simultaneously. Leadership creates the conditions in schools where all learners grow, progress, graduate, go on to some form of post-secondary learning and lead productive lives. It is our central belief that regardless of the innovative structures and new forms of schooling that are developed, the strongest forms of schooling will be characterized by trusting relationships and the development of outstanding learning by professionally connected and supported teachers.

In the next chapter, you will meet Alison, a new principal with intense moral purpose working in a small elementary school in a rural community. You will explore this first mindset as you consider the broad purposes of schooling, think about what quality really means, imagine new forms of quality in your context and reflect on how ethics, passion and commitment are at the heart of leadership. You will also consider issues of school identity and sustainability and you will follow Alison's journey as a new school leader doing her best to create quality and equity for learners.

Questions for consideration

1   Think about leaders – formal or informal – you respect for the difference they are making to the learning of individuals and to groups of learners within their schools. To what extent do they reflect the growth mindset described by Carol Dweck?

2   Shifting schools from sorting to learning systems is central to the new work of school leaders. Think about your own school. In what ways are you making these fundamental shifts? In what areas do you think you need more concentrated effort?

3   Education has no shortage of proposed reforms or innovations. *So Much Reform So Little Change* (2008) is the title of a recently published book by American writer Charles Payne. This title is an accurate description in many educational settings because many of us have all too frequently seen well-intentioned reforms flounder for one reason or another. Think about the innovations you have seen that resulted in real change in your setting. What conditions led to this success? What are the implications for you as a leader?

Note

1   For more information on the application of positive deviance in public health, please see http://www.positivedeviance.org.

Chapter 2

Intense moral purpose

> Those in positions of responsibility – educational leaders –
> have to carry the burdens of being proactively responsible for
> changing those things which they have some control over in
> order to alleviate disadvantage and promote the deeply human
> fulfillment of young people.
>
> Robert Starratt (2004, p. 144)
> *Ethical Leadership*
>
> People are passionate about things, issues, causes and people.
> Being passionate generates energy, determination, conviction,
> commitment and even obsession. Passion is not a luxury, a frill
> or a quality possessed by just a few principals. It is essential to
> sustaining successful leadership.
>
> Christopher Day and Kenneth Leithwood (eds) (2007, p. 176)
> *Successful Principal Leadership in Times of Change:*
> *An International Perspective.*

*Alison MacDonald had been a teacher in her small northern community for
many years. Her community has struggled with the long-term impact of
residential schooling*[1] *– racism, unemployment, poverty and abuse. She has
regularly taken in foster children and she has provided the kind of constant
love and support in her primary classroom that many families struggled to
provide at home. She has used her own resources to help students continue their
education after graduation. She has developed and maintains lifetime friendships with her students and their families. The community respect Alison for
her commitment to quality learning and they value the opportunities she
provides for seniors to share their experiences and knowledge with her young*

learners. As part of the school science programme, her learners have developed knowledge about local plants, herbs and wildlife from elders. She has also championed the arts at Evergreen School and, as a result, every year her learners have the opportunity to incorporate visual and performing arts into a school opera. When the headship became vacant in her school, Alison was reluctant to apply. Her plate was already full with her work as a teacher leader within the union, her work as a literacy coach and her countless hours of volunteer work outside of school. Nevertheless, she had seen the impact of school leaders who sincerely believed in the potential of vulnerable learners and she knew all too well the negative effect of leaders who saw only limitations and obstacles. Finally, with the urging of her teacher colleagues, Alison applied. At first tentative in this new role, she soon became a passionately committed and effective leader.

Karim Jaafer is the principal of Lindsay Creek Secondary School. Lindsay Creek is located in a downtown area adjacent to a refugee settlement centre. For many of the students from Sub-Saharan Africa, Kosovo, Afghanistan and other war-torn parts of the world, this is their first experience in school. They come with a history of trauma and often with little or no literacy skills in their native languages let alone in English. The school provides them with a sense of security and community – and they learn. At the same time as they are immersed in English language instruction and are supported in their academic learning, their mothers access food, clothing and companionship at the school. Local cooperatives have been set up to help the women become more self-sufficient. They see the school as a place where their dreams for their children are realized. Karim knows from his first-hand experience the important role that school plays in providing a hand-up to young people whose lives have been so extraordinarily difficult. He is proud of the teachers who go far beyond the limits of subject or curriculum to touch the lives of these new learners and he is deeply moved at graduation when he sees them cross the stage with a diploma and a future in their hands.

Alison and Karim are leaders with intense moral purpose. They are determined to improve the life chances of their learners by working with their colleagues and their community to provide young people with the highest possible quality learning experience. Alison values the traditional measures of educational quality such as competency in literacy and mathematics and she also knows how important it is to expand the concept of quality to include the arts, imagination, creativity, citizenship and social responsibility. She is working hard to develop a strong identity for her school and she is concerned about capacity building so that the professional learning work of her school can be sustained over time. Karim knows the difference his school can make and he also knows that the impact the teachers are making on the lives of their students will never show up on the media-touted school rankings.

In every discussion we have had with teachers, parents and learners about what makes an effective leader, passion is always close to or at the top of the list. Christopher Day and Ken Leithwood's (2007) synthesis of international studies of highly successful leaders confirms this observation. They found that a passionate commitment to making a difference to young people they served was a common characteristic. It is this passion, this 'fire in the belly', that keeps leaders focused on creating success for all learners even when the odds seemed stacked against them. This same quality of passion was evident in a case study of successful leaders in the United Kingdom (Day and Hatfield, 2005). These leaders were working in an accountability environment considered by the researchers to be highly test-oriented. Nonetheless, they were able to manage ongoing and competing tensions in developing a strong programme for learners by focusing on their own values and moral purpose. They were not afraid to fail or to acknowledge their failure and they would not give up. These leaders made sure that they learned from what did not work the first time. Their deeply held values and their strong sense of purpose allowed them to seek, synthesize and evaluate evidence from sources both inside and outside their school communities. They actively sought out and used this range of resources first to understand and then to solve their school problems. They faced challenges head on and persevered in their work towards an equitable future for their students.

As school leaders ourselves, we have faced the challenges inherent in creating stronger learning cultures and we know the importance of courage and perseverance. School leadership is not for the faint of heart. We know changing school cultures is hard work and we also know that it is good and satisfying work. We know the rewards that come when learners of all ages begin to see themselves as capable, confident and hopeful. In this chapter, we will explore the implications for leaders who are passionately focused on quality and equity. We will look at the broad purposes of education and the connections of these purposes with quality, equity and ethics. We will consider the leader's role in developing school identity and building sustainability. As you consider these ideas, think about the leaders you admire and respect. Think about your own motivation for leadership and think about the learners you serve.

Broad purposes for education

Alison and Karim are proud of their schools and the differences they are making. The recent school musical at Evergreen involved every child from kindergarten to Year 7. The pleasure on their faces as they sang and danced their way through the multiple performances and the pride of their parents and grandparents, dissolved the fatigue from endless hours of rehearsal. The weekly cross-grade coaching that several classes were involved in was paying off not only in improving the reading comprehension of her learners, but also in the way the older and younger children interacted on the playground and on the long daily bus ride. The vegetable and flower garden the staff, families and children had planted was in full bloom. The school regularly made contributions of fresh flowers to the local seniors' centre and the children were enjoying incorporating fresh produce into their lunch programme. She knew how hard the teachers worked and how much they cared. It disturbed her that teachers were discouraged each year when the league tables were printed in the paper. No league table or ranking would ever be able to reflect the heart and spirit in her school.

At Lindsay Creek, teachers were determined that not only would their new learners get the learning support they needed to graduate and to go on to post-secondary education. They also knew the importance of building a renewed sense of hope and community. Every learner new to the school had an adult advocate in the school as long as it was necessary. Whether the custodian, the Physics teacher, or the cafeteria supervisor, with Karim's leadership and modelling, virtually every adult was making a personal connection with learners. Adults took the time to explore the talents and interests of these newcomers and there was always a way to cover the fees, travel or uniform costs so that they could participate on a team or in a club. The new students were also encouraged to contribute their time and talents to helping others. Learners were actively involved in projects like Habitat for Humanity where they not only learned trade skills; they also learned teamwork and contribution.

We have found that our strongest leaders have an expansive view of the kind of education they want for young people in their schools. Although they understand the importance to the public of success on consistent measures of achievement, they have a much broader conception of what is meant by learning and quality. They work relentlessly to promote a generous and enlarged conception of learning success for their learners and for their schools. Some of the school leaders we work with have read *Learning, the Treasure Within*, the Delors Report (1996) commissioned by UNESCO, but most have not. Their personal philosophies, however, match the thinking of the authors who describe a broad and rich education as desirable for young people around the world.

The international group of authors who wrote the report described four foundations for a global educational framework to be used by educators and citizens in thinking about individual and system life-long learning. These foundations are learning to live together, learning to be, learning to know and learning to do. In our experience, school leaders with strong moral purpose want their learners to grow in all of these areas. School leaders like Alison and Karim spend considerable time thinking about and developing an understanding of local and global citizenship with their staff and learners.

Learning to live together

We agree with the emphasis in the United Nations report on the critical importance of young people learning to live together. The successful school leaders we have studied believe that when learners develop an understanding of other people and their history, traditions, culture and spiritual values, an appreciation for diverse perspectives and a new spirit of international connectedness can be created:

> Creating a new spirit which, guided by recognition of our growing interdependence and a common analysis of the risks and challenges of the future, would induce people to implement common projects or to manage the inevitable conflicts in an intelligent and peaceful way. Utopia, some may think, but it is a necessary Utopia, indeed a vital one if we are to escape from a dangerous cycle sustained by cynicism or by resignation.
>
> (1996, p. 20)

Leaders with intense moral purpose understand that learning to live together is critically important work in schools since, in the years that have passed since the Delors Report was written, our collective understanding has only deepened about how essential learning to live together is to global survival.

Learning to be

An earlier (1972) UNESCO report, *Learning to Be*, expressed fears about the possible dehumanizing effects of technology. The 1996 report noted that technological progress and the enlarged power of global media makes the importance of developing thoughtful and reflective citizens even more critical. Central to the intense moral purpose mindset is the leader's role in ensuring that every learner is able to enjoy the freedom of thought, judgment, feeling and imagination to develop their talents and control as much of their lives as they can (1996: 1).

The impact of high stakes accountability systems in many parts of the world has led to significant concerns about reductionism in curriculum and limitations on creativity and imagination. The Delors Report includes cautions about the impacts of global economic and social changes and suggests that imagination and creativity must be accorded a special place:

> The clearest expressions of human freedom (imagination and creativity) may be threatened by the establishment of a certain degree of uniformity in individual behaviour. The twenty-first century will need a varied range of talents and personalities even more than exceptionally gifted individuals, who are equally essential in any society . . . At school, art and poetry should take a much more important place than they are given in many countries by an education that has become more utilitarian than cultural. Concern with developing the imagination and creativity should also restore the value of oral culture and knowledge drawn from children's or adults' experiences.
>
> (1996: pp. 1–2)

As we look at recent trends in school systems, we are encouraged by the renewed focus on the arts, creativity, active health and imagination in many places previously focused exclusively on narrower definitions of quality. We hope these trends will gain even greater momentum. School leaders with intense moral purpose have always found ways to avoid being constrained in their views of quality. Alison's commitment to developing the oral language skills and artistic abilities of her young learners is simply one example of this more generous-spirited view of learning. Karim's determination to create a sense of community and support for new learners and their families is another. We need more leaders like them.

Learning to know

School leaders understand that it is important for young people to develop skills in learning to know. This involves both the acquisition of structured knowledge and the development of cognitive learning tools. Learning can be viewed both as a means to an end and as an end in itself. Considering learning as a means suggests that people have to learn to understand the world around them, at least as much as is necessary for them to lead their lives with some dignity, develop their occupational skills and communicate with other people. Regarded as an end, learning is connected with the pleasure that is derived from understanding, knowledge and discovery. We have found that our strongest school leaders value both purposes of learning and take delight themselves in learning and in the learning of those around them.

Learning to know also implies learning how to learn by developing one's concentration and ability to think. As forms of work become increasingly less routine, the ability to problem solve and to engage in abstract thought becomes even more important as a lifelong skill. A focus on learning to know means that leaders must pay attention to the conceptions of learning that are considered important in their school context. Are teachers driven by a pressure – real or self-imposed – to 'cover the curriculum'? Are lessons and units endlessly repeated because of teacher preference and interest or are they designed to meet the deep learning needs of the students? Do learning experiences incorporate imagination, metacognition, teamwork, abstract reasoning and complex, challenging real world problems? In schools with strong leadership, the answers to these questions are generally 'yes'.

Learning to do

The fourth foundation, learning to do, involves the acquisition of competencies that enable people to deal with a variety of situations, most of which are unforeseeable. Learning to do also involves the ability to work purposefully and cooperatively in teams and recognizes that the failure to be successful as an employee is more often related to a lack of interpersonal skills than a lack of technical skills. Competence in teamwork and related interpersonal skills are more readily acquired if students have the opportunity to try out and develop their abilities by becoming involved in work experiences or service learning programmes while they are still in school. Alison's cross-grade coaching programme, in place even with very young learners, provides the opportunity for the kind of teamwork, mentoring, coaching, reflection and planning that is involved in young people learning to do. All the young people at Lindsay Creek are involved in community service learning. The skills and the connections they make by working side by side with community mentors are invaluable.

Learning to respect the natural world

Since the publication of the Delors Report in 1996, there has been a growing number of thinkers, including Andy Hargreaves and Dean Fink (2006) who, while acknowledging the importance of these four foundations, have called for the addition of a fifth foundation, that of young people learning to respect the natural world by learning to live in a more sustainable manner. Indigenous educational leaders such as Lorna Williams (2006) point out that understanding the natural world from an indigenous perspective and developing a deeper respect for the natural world are critically important to human survival (2006: 11). The complexity of environmental issues confronting learners as global citizens is connected with attitudes, knowledge and action. We need young people who can understand and make sense of complex issues and reach an informed opinion. The broader our knowledge base, the better we can understand the many different aspects of our environment. The Delors Report noted that studying environmental issues encourages greater intellectual curiosity, sharpens the critical faculties and enables people to develop their own independent judgements on the world around them (1996: 1). From the perspective of nurturing the health of the natural world, a strong education in inquiry and active local and global citizenship are critically important to all learners, no matter where they live.

Alison's efforts to build the wisdom of the older people in her community into the science programme at her school and the school's efforts to build and maintain a community garden are helping learners gain respect for the natural world. Through their community service learning projects, Karim's learners are starting to see their world in a different way and are learning that it is their responsibility to become involved and make a contribution to their community – both locally and globally.

Reimagining quality

We believe that there is a continuing need for learning connected with the traditional conceptions of quality. We also believe that new conceptions and measures of quality are required. Many leaders are working in schools where achievement in literacy, mathematics and science are predominantly valued and are 'counted' for accountability purposes. Few school leaders would disagree with the priority placed on the ability to read, write, speak, listen and problem-solve. Evidence about the important influence of early literacy success on lifelong learning and positive health outcomes has only helped to reinforce the importance of these priorities. Acquiring and using knowledge has been and will remain important.

Learning to live together, to be, to do and to respect the natural world are all newer forms of quality, in the sense that few school systems in the world have made these broader priorities an explicit part of their policy environments. New forms of technology have created an interest in and a demand for an expanded understanding of what is meant by literacy. Social networking and easy access to a wealth of information via the Internet places demands on individuals to be discerning in their choices. School leaders with moral purpose are paying close attention to multiple literacies and forms of intelligence.

The attitudinal survey data from PISA[2] (Program for International Student Assessment) paint a disappointing picture of students' current engagement and satisfaction with their learning experiences. The report suggests that close to half of all secondary learners across the countries studied (and regardless of their achievement levels) are disengaged in school and are going through the motions of learning with an externally motivated, performativity habit of mind. This disengagement of adolescent learners underlines once more the need for a shift from schools focused on sorting to systems passionate about deep learning. We have seen learner engagement increase as schools become more innovative and responsive and much less 'school as usual'. New forms and uses of technology, greater personalization, imaginative forms of learning engagement, the use of learning how to learn strategies, deep and supportive relationships and new forms of learning-oriented structures are being developed – and are required.

Reimagining quality requires leaders to reconsider what is valued in their schools. How are learners recognized for their contributions?

Where is time and attention most often invested? Are teachers encouraged and supported for risk-taking and innovation? Are parents and community members well informed of the range of learning opportunities in the school or is their only source of information the league tables and media rankings? Are schools like the ones Alison and Karim lead recognized for the impact that they are having on addressing issues of both quality and equity?

Equity and ethics

In some of her darker moments, Alison remembered a comment made by Jack, a former district leader, who had said that the children in her village would never succeed. He wrote off a whole generation of children because he could not see beyond their economic poverty and was unable to imagine a better future. Every time she thought of this comment, Alison felt angry. How dare he judge the future of her learners by their current circumstances! She remembered her own Grade 7 teacher telling her that she wasn't smart enough to go to college. It was only through her own steely resolve that she had proven this teacher wrong. Alison knew that focusing on oral language and early literacy skills was essential for her youngest learners. She found creative ways to provide support for her learners during the summer and also to equip family members with the strategies they needed to help their young readers develop a love of reading. She believed in the potential of the school in playing a role in cracking the cycle of poverty. It was important to her to prove that Jack was wrong.

Whenever he got discouraged, Karim remembered Mr Bert, his Physical Education teacher in Year 8. Karim had been a skinny kid with limited English skills who hadn't had a chance to play organized sports. He loved the action in the gym and started hanging around after school watching the older boys practise. One day Mr Bert tossed him a ball and showed him how to do a jump shot. He was hooked and from that moment on he spent every spare moment in the gym. Mr Bert patiently worked with him and it wasn't too long before Karim had a spot on the junior team. With steady encouragement from his coach, Karim started to take on a leadership role on the court and in the school. When Karim was struggling in Mathematics, Mr Bert arranged extra help for him. Karim wondered if he would have ever dreamed of becoming a teacher, let alone a principal, if it were not for this teacher who believed in him.

The leaders we have observed and those profiled in the Day and Leithwood (2007) study understand that they are leading schools with the potential to create more equitable futures for their learners.

They are interested in making a difference to valued long-term outcomes such as intergenerational mobility. A report for the Sutton Trust (2005) defines this equity area:

> The level of intergenerational mobility in society is seen by many as a measure of the extent of equality of economic opportunity or life chances. It captures the extent to which a person's circumstances during childhood are reflected in their success in later life.
>
> (p. 1)

We have worked with many leaders like Alison and Karim who are fierce in their determination to make sure that children, regardless of their families' circumstances, get the experiences and opportunities they need to complete secondary education and to access post secondary programmes. These leaders are intensely focused on ensuring their learners can experience lifetime learning success and healthier lives as community members and citizens. They want to help build a system that allows for and creates mobility over the generations so that young people – all young people – can have better lives and make productive contributions to their families and to society.

In the knowledge society, it is no longer acceptable or sufficient for education systems to sort learners into those who pass and those who fail, those who can go on to post-secondary opportunities and those who cannot. Young people need to develop a sense of belonging, a sense of well-being, a sense of civic engagement and a sense that they have a wide range of capabilities. They need to be able to live, learn and contribute locally and globally. Across the globe, policy-makers are looking to education systems – to schools – to create these opportunities and to be more responsive to the diversity of their learners. UNESCO in their report (2000) about education for all learners, challenged the international educational community to reach six big learning goals by 2015:

- growing and improving comprehensive early childhood care and education, especially for the most vulnerable and disadvantaged children;
- ensuring that all children, particularly girls, children in difficult circumstances and those belonging to minorities, have access to and complete, free and compulsory primary education of good quality;

- ensuring that the learning needs of all young people and adults are met through equitable access to appropriate learning and life skills programmes;
- achieving a 50 per cent improvement in levels of adult literacy, especially for women and more equitable access for all adults;
- achieving gender equality in participation in good quality primary and secondary education; and
- improving all aspects of the quality of education and ensuring excellence of all so that recognized and measurable outcomes are achieved by all, especially in literacy, numeracy and essential life skills (2000, p. 8).

The 2008 Global Monitoring Report on Education For All[3] indicates that progress has been made on these goals but that this progress is uneven. As Tony Townsend (2007) points out in the concluding chapter of *The International Handbook of School Improvement and Effectiveness*, many systems in developed as well as developing countries would have difficulty in demonstrating that they are currently meeting all of these equity goals (2007, p. 952). International results from PISA and UNESCO studies provide pictures of quality and equity on a national level. This kind of information can open up important discussions about how education needs to improve and can generate significant policy decisions. At the school level, leaders with intense moral purpose are also asking questions related to quality and equity goals such as those raised by UNESCO. Conceptions of quality and equity are not abstractions for school leaders such as Alison and Karim. They are very real and drive their day-to-day actions.

Implication for school leaders

Alison's passion for quality and equity required her to question and then confront some long held traditions in her school. She questioned whether the delivery of special education was truly reflecting the most current knowledge and practice for meeting the needs of vulnerable learners. She knew that raising this issue would cause a lot of concern with her colleagues and she knew she would find it difficult to live with herself unless changes were made. She took a hard look at the performance of her students and this analysis confirmed her suspicions that there was a gap in reading comprehension and fluency between the boys and the girls. She became a vociferous advocate for new resources and strategies that would appeal to the boys.

Although Alison loved her school, she started to look at it through the eyes of families new to the community and wondered whether it was truly as welcoming and inclusive as she believed. Alison knew the importance of a sense of identity and how for many of her learners, being part of a strong school community provided them with an important sense of belonging and purpose. She smiled as she recalled overhearing one of her Year 1 learners proudly saying to her parents, 'I'm going to like going to Evergreen because everyone here is a writer and an artist.'

Despite the many successes that Lindsay Creek was having in creating hopeful futures for their new learners, Karim was aware that some teachers were worried about the end of course exams and their own reputations when the results were publicized. He wanted to make sure these teachers had the support they needed to deepen their focus on learning and success for every learner and not feel threatened by the newspaper reports. Although Karim knew how important sustained leadership was for his school, he had been told that the district would move him within a year or two to another school. He was determined to build capacity in others on staff so that the culture they were building would be strengthened and sustained.

Leadership in schools is about making a difference in the lives of all learners regardless of their family background, socioeconomic status, race, gender, sexual orientation, or geographic location. School leadership involves increasing the learning of all students as well as closing any 'gap' between groups of students. A quick glance at the PISA results shows that Canada is one of the top performing countries in terms of both quality and equity. There is more to this story, however. Despite some recent improvements, there is still a significant gap across Canada in the success of Aboriginal learners and increasingly there is concern about how newcomers from some parts of the world are faring in Canadian secondary schools. In the province of British Columbia, focused attention is beginning to be paid to the learning needs of children in care – a population that was virtually invisible, until a determined child advocate[4] began examining the performance evidence and identifying the discrepancies. Advocates for children would agree with Fullan (2003) who contends that these learners need school leaders who are:

> immersed in disciplined, informed professional inquiry and action that results in raising the bar and closing the gap by engaging all students in learning. There is no greater moral imperative than revamping the principal's role as part and parcel

of changing the context within which teachers teach and students learn.

(p. 11)

Our strongest leaders are working hard to close any gaps in performance and are deeply concerned about the needs of their most vulnerable learners. They are persistent in their efforts to create more even learning 'playing fields' so that every young person can do well. Vulnerability, a term first used by Doug Willms (2003), implies that circumstances for individual learners can improve through learner and educator effort, with school and community support.

School leaders with intense moral purpose for quality and equity, must be informed by an honest appraisal of how well the school is serving the needs of vulnerable learners. Leaders look critically at the available evidence of learning, especially as it connects with underserved groups and learners from challenging circumstances. Ignoring some of the more 'brutal' realities for learners is not an option. Listening deeply to learners about their experiences with poverty, racism, homophobia or sexism not only builds respect and understanding, it also fuels the fire of moral purpose. Honestly confronting our areas of weakness and failure, as well as understanding and building on our current strengths, are essential.

Despite the rhetoric about caring about learner success, not all schools place the needs of their learners at the heart of their work. Sometimes through history, a lack of awareness or a lack of courage, schools and whole systems have developed cultures more attuned to the desires of the adults than the learning needs of the young people attending school. Changing cultures that have been developed for the convenience of the adults, rather than for the imperative of creating positive life chances for every learner, requires leaders with passion, intensity, persistence and ethical drive.

Ethical practice, passion and purpose

Robert Starratt (2004), after considering the nature of ethical leadership for many years across a range of settings, has concluded that ethical educators need to combine three key virtues – the virtues of responsibility, presence and authenticity. Starratt claims:

> What differentiates exceptional educational leaders from their colleagues is the intensity and depth with which they exercise these virtues in their work. Their role as educators necessarily

involves their humanity as well as their role as citizens. The work of education is a deeply human work and it is intrinsically a work of citizenship as well. The authentic and responsible educator is one whose own authenticity is channeled and poured out in authentic relationships with learners, in authentic relationship to the activity of learning itself and in authentic relationship to the human, academic and civic curriculum that constitutes the joint work with student-learners.

(2004: p. 106)

The ethical qualities that Starratt describes are what make the work of school leadership simultaneously so challenging and so rewarding. Leaders face dilemmas every day in their pursuit of a higher quality and more equitable learning world. They balance the tensions between applying an ethic of care and an ethic of justice as they work with individual learners and the school community as a whole. They bring to life an ethic of critique as they engage in interactions with staff, learners and families, making sure that the vulnerable learners get fair treatment and that the needs and wants of more privileged learners do not automatically prevail.

The strongest leaders model a strong ethic of professionalism with an intense and practical focus on what is best for individual learners as well as what is best for the community of learners. Considering and understanding varied ethical perspectives demands leaders who have strong cognitive skills as well as a clear sense of personal values. A well-developed sense of personal identity can help school leaders when they are confronting difficult ethical decisions. The development of a strong school identity gives meaning and direction to the lives of faculty, learners and their families.

Developing a school identity

School leaders have long been exhorted to create a strong school vision or mission. We have seen too many schools spend an inordinate amount of time developing lofty mission statements and compelling vision statements that all too frequently have become not worth much more than the glossy paper on which they have been written. The notion of school identity is more action-oriented and tangible. Alison's determination to create a sense of identity at Evergreen as a 'writing school', a school where the arts are valued and celebrated and a school where the indigenous wisdom of elders is honoured is a reflection of her moral purpose in action. Lindsay Creek was becoming well-known for its success in creating strong learners and strong citizens from amongst the refugee population. With its innovative use of technology and range of supports available to learners and their families, Lindsay Creek was referred to as a school where learners really got a chance and where diversity was not just tolerated, but celebrated.

James Spillane, Emily Benz and Elisa Mandel (2004) provide some useful perspectives on the role of the leader in creating strong and unique school identities. In *The Stories Schools Live By*, Spillane and his colleagues describe school identity as an internalized cognitive structure of what the school stands for and where it intends to go:

> [I]dentity is especially relevant when it comes to an organization's capacity to learn and innovate. Scholars argue that while organizations can engage in minor changes to their existing routines without changing their identity, fundamental change in an organization's routines necessitates changes in organizational identity.
>
> (2004, p. 4)

As schools move from a sorting orientation to deep learning for all, a fundamental change in the identity of the school is required. A relatively simple identity-oriented question for any school leader is to consider the entrance and interior organization of their school building. Is there consistency between what the school says it values and what can be seen in the school? Is the first impression given to learners, families and visitors entering the school one of an intense focus on learning? Are there displays of student learning connected with this focus and are at least some of the displays at the eye level of the learners? What does the allocation of learning spaces say about what the school values? Are new teachers relegated to the most unappealing spaces until they outlive or outlast teachers with the 'best' classrooms? Are learners with special needs in attractive learning spaces or are they hidden away in some dark corner of the building? Are display cases gathering dust with relics of a bygone era?

School identity, as we conceptualize it, is not focused primarily on choice or competition. It is about every school creating a positive distinctiveness that builds pride for learners and their communities. We expect all leaders to be able to talk with pride about the identity of their own school – and of all other schools in their district or community. Parents want to have confidence in their children's school and in the system as a whole. We have been influenced by the thinking of Darrell Bricker and Edward Greenspon (2002), in their book *Searching for Certainty: The New Canadian Mindset* as they claim that Canadians are much less interested in the ranking of schools than in knowing that every school is a good school.

It is our observation that schools that develop a strong learning identity regarding the growth of both the intellect and character of their learners also seem to have secured the confidence of their local community. We have seen a small rural school combine its skills in filmmaking and cross-country skiing to forge a unique identity and to generate considerable interest and support from residents and families in neighboring villages. At a middle school serving a large immigrant community, it has become a tradition for every student to research and prepare a multi-media presentation on a topic of special interest to their parents and accessible to them in their own language. Topics include requirements for a driving licence, understanding the tax system, obtaining health benefits, or preparing a CV. Schools like Lindsay Creek that have made service learning a way of life as a result are positively changing the interactions between community members and adolescents. School leaders sometimes use their own passions and talents to create a stronger school identity. We admire the experienced principal who was able to take her own love of dance and music and create a robust performing arts identity in a remote community. Other urban school leaders have built on the strength of their technology resources to create innovative and responsive programmes that shape the school's identity. Many schools have embraced environmental education and healthy living and are strengthening their school's identity as a result.

Whether it is a focus on healthy living, technological innovation, the arts, science, the environment, oral story telling, service learning, or outdoor recreation – the possibilities are numerous and are limited only by the imagination of the school leader and the staff. Once a strong identity has been established, it also must be sustained until it truly becomes 'a way of life' that leads to changes in learning and in the experiences of the learners. Once the visible change in learning becomes part of a new school story, the new identity creates a sense of renewed purpose. Spillane and colleagues note in their paper:

> School reformers often dwell on how new structures, routines and tools can enable schools to learn and change in order to

improve student achievement. We argue that while structures, routines and tools are critical, they are unlikely to be sufficient on their own; they need a compass, a sense of purpose. We suggest based on our analysis that organizational identity as embodied in the story that teachers and administrators tell about their school may serve as that compass.

(p. 38)

If school identity provides a moral compass as Spillane suggests, then leaders must also be concerned with issues of sustainability. What will happen when the formal leader leaves? Will the work continue? Will the identity of the school continue to provide a sense of purpose and direction?

Sustainability and purpose

Part of a leader's responsibility is to develop a clear direction for the school. As part of direction-setting, leaders pay attention to the unique and positive identity for the school and they exercise their leadership in such a way that the momentum is sustained over time. Karim and Alison are aware of what might happen after they leave their school. As leaders with moral purpose they consider the issues of sustainability from their first moments in their schools. Will the improvements and the changes they have initiated continue after they leave? Will their schools become genuinely transformed centres of learning?

From personal experience, we can appreciate the disappointment and cynicism that arises when initiatives are not sustained after a change in formal leadership. A staff can only hold a course or direction for so long, without the support and involvement of the formal leader. Hargreaves and Fink (2006) spent many years researching reform implementation in a number of Canadian and American schools and from this study they developed seven principles for sustainable leadership that are directly connected to moral purpose. They suggest that school leaders need to ensure that leadership lasts by creating meaningful changes and planning for the future. They talk about the importance of breadth when they say that leadership spreads by developing the identity and direction of the school collectively and by distributing leadership. They emphasize the need to be socially just so that all students and other schools benefit. Further, they recommend that leaders exercise resourcefulness by providing intrinsic rewards and extrinsic incentives, allow time and opportunity for professional learning development, be cost effective without being cheap and carefully handle resources to support all learners. From their perspective, leaders promote diversity to enable educators and families to adapt and prosper in increasingly complex environments by learning from one another's diverse practices. Leaders are activists in engaging assertively with the educational environment in a pattern of mutual influence, activating personal and professional networks and forming strategic alliances. Their final principle is that leaders ensure school and system support for sustainable leadership by developing improvements that last over time – by distributing leadership and responsibility to others and by sustaining themselves so that they can persist with their vision and avoid burning out (adapted from 2006, pp. 1–7).

Taking seriously the principles of sustainability as described by Hargreaves and Fink (2006) is work that frequently goes beyond the scope of the individual principal. District, provincial, state and national leaders need to be very careful that in their enthusiasm for new initiatives or in their desire to respond to a variety of demands, they do not work against sustainability by moving school leaders too quickly. We have seen in our case study schools the churn that occurs when leaders are shuffled too frequently. Rapid turnover works directly against moral purpose. Moving schools to deep learning requires sustained effort.

Conclusion

Leading the shift away from a sorting system where there is success for some towards a learning system where there is deep learning for all is at the heart of moral purpose. School leaders committed to this new work understand that they must build on the existing quality of their school, create new forms of quality and be persistent in their drive for equity. Leaders help to build a strong sense of school identity, are brutally honest in their appraisal of their school's strengths, create a sense of direction and pay attention to the importance of sustainability.

In addition to an individual leader's mindset of intense moral purpose, this is work that also requires cooperation, collaboration and teamwork. Individual teachers working in isolation cannot be expected to meet the needs of every learner. The work is simply too hard and a team approach is required. The same case can be made for schools and for school leaders. School leaders who are passionate about learning and improvement know that they must build a strong team both within and outside the school. This requires high levels of trust and emotional intelligence. In the next chapter we will explore the impact of trust on learning and follow Chris, a secondary principal, as he strives to build trust in a school where relationships have been damaged.

Questions for consideration

1   To what extent are the four foundations of learning to live together, learning to know, learning to be and learning to do integral parts of the learning programme at your school? To what extent is learning to respect the natural world a way of life at your school?
2   What progress is your school making in simultaneously moving towards high quality and greater equity? What are your greatest strengths in these two areas?
3   What difference do you think having a strong identity makes for a school – especially for a school serving vulnerable learners? Does your school have a strong learning-focused identity? How did this develop? What will you do to sustain it? Does this identity need to be adapted to incorporate new forms of quality? If there isn't a strong learning identity in your school, what steps will you take to build one?
4   What forms of quality are currently valued in your school? What new forms of quality do you believe would help strengthen the experiences of learners – and the confidence of their parents – in your school?
5   Who are the learners you are most concerned about in your school? What are you doing as a school to better meet their needs?

Notes

1   For several decades in Canada, Aboriginal children were removed from their homes and placed in residential schools. On June 11 2008, the Prime Minister Stephen Harper, issued a formal apology to First Nations' peoples for this practice. The last residential school closed in 1996.
2   www.pisa.oecd.org
3   http://eunedoc.unesco.org/images/0015001548/154820e.pdf.
4   Mary Ellen Turpel-Lafond Representative for Children and Youth.

Chapter 3

Trust – relationships first

Principals' actions play a key role in developing and sustaining relational trust. Principals establish both trust and personal regard when they acknowledge the vulnerabilities of others, actively listen to their concerns and eschew arbitrary actions. Effective principals couple these behaviors with a compelling school vision and behavior that clearly seeks to advance the vision. This consistency between words and actions affirms their personal integrity. Then, if the principal competently manages basic day-to-day school affairs, an overall ethos conducive to the formation of trust will emerge.

Anthony Bryk and Barbara Schneider (2003, p. 43)
Trust in Schools; A Core Resource for School Reform.

School leaders need to view trust as the bridge that reform must be carried over, but rather than being solid, that bridge is built on changing emotions.

Karen Seashore Louis (2007, p. 20)
Trust and Improvement in Schools.
Journal of Educational Change.

Chris Vanderhoven was looking forward with both anticipation and some trepidation to meeting the staff, the parents and the learners at Riverbank Secondary School. A relatively large school with 1400 students in Years 8–12, Riverbank was located in a mixed income urban area with a growing immigrant and refugee population. From his experience in the district, Chris was well aware of the school's reputation. It was described sarcastically by educators in the district as a centre of excellence for ethics charges, with strained relationships both among staff and between staff and parents being the norm. While there were pockets of excellence – the chef-training and music programmes were exemplary – the overall sense was that Riverbank was a sinking school.

Student suspensions were high and success rates were low. The previous principal, Leo, had been seen as more involved in developing his personal interests than in improving the school. After two years in the school, Leo had been transferred. As a new principal, Chris knew that one of his key priorities was to build trust. He needed to shift the school's story from one of cynicism and negativity to one of hope and determination. Just how that would happen, he was less sure.

Strong levels of trust and respectful relationships are preconditions for successful school improvement initiatives. When adult relationships in schools are characterized by trust, the stories about change shift from indifference or negativity to possibility and hope. John Kotter (2002) argues for the importance of relationships and social and emotional understanding. He points out that clear thinking is an essential part of large-scale change and that identifying the appropriate strategy for change is crucial. No change strategy, however, works without sufficient attention being paid to the quality of relationships and the level of trust:

> Clear thinking is a critical part of large-scale change, whether in a big organization or a small department. Figuring out the right strategy is perhaps the most obvious example. Locating information to be used in raising urgency is another. Selecting possibilities for short-term wins is still another. But look at story after story of highly successful change methods and you find a pattern that is closer to the heart of the matter. People are sensitive to the emotions that undermine change and they find ways to reduce those feelings. People are sensitive to the emotions that facilitate change and they find ways to enhance those feelings.
>
> (p. 180)

Karen Seashore Louis (2006) maintains that the key to shifting school cultures in a positive way involves developing and combining three critical elements: professional community, organizational learning and trust. She concludes that of these three elements, trust must come first: 'Trust is a precondition for developing professional learning communities, but few schools (and probably fewer school administrators) have confronted the issue of how to improve this component of organizational functioning' (p. 483). As well, Solomon and Flores (2001) argue that 'trust is cultivated through speech, conversation, commitments and action. Trust is never something 'already at hand', it is always a matter of human effort. It can and often must be conscientiously created, not simply taken for granted' (p. 87).

In previous studies, trust has been defined as the shared understanding by the entire staff that both the staff itself and the individuals within the staff are reliable – that they can be counted on to do what they say they will do (Tschannen-Moran and Hoy 1998; Hoy and Tschannen-Moran 1999). Further consideration of the concept resulted in a description of five components of staff trust: benevolence, honesty, openness, reliability and competence (Tschannen-Moran 2004).

Benevolence is defined as confidence that one's well-being will be protected. Honesty concerns a person's character, integrity and authenticity. Openness is the process by which people make themselves vulnerable to others by sharing information, influence and control. Reliability reflects the idea that any staff member can be counted on to help and competence is seen as the demonstrated ability to deliver on the promises being made.

As principals, we have experienced first hand the challenges in and the importance of building trust in our own schools. We have seen in our case study schools many powerful examples of the impact – both positive and negative – that leaders can have on trust levels in their schools. In this chapter, we will describe how a mindset focused on trusting relationships is fundamental to creating positive learning change. We will follow Chris in his efforts to transform his school to illustrate the specific components of trust and to describe the ways in which school leaders build trust and reduce the negative emotions that undermine the conditions for positive change.

Why relational trust is essential to learning

Most educators we work with acknowledge that they consider trusting relationships to be important in creating positive school cultures. Fewer are able to identify the key role trust plays in actually improving student learning. New and experienced leaders have appreciated the findings from a longitudinal study on the impact of trust in Chicago schools as they reflect on the development of relational trust in their own schools. Researchers Anthony Bryk and Barbara Schneider (2003) identified relational trust as a key variable in increasing student learning:

> A school with a low score on relational trust at the end of our study had only a one-in-seven chance of demonstrating improved academic productivity. In contrast, half of the schools that scored high on relational trust were in the improved group. On average, these improving schools recorded increases in student learning of 8 percent in reading and 20 percent in Mathematics in a five-year period.

(p. 43)

Bryk and Schneider (2002, 2003) identified four key components of trusting relationships: respect, personal regard, personal integrity and competence in core responsibilities. When these four dimensions of trust were in place, parents, staff and the leadership team were able to work effectively to increase safety, belonging and learning. The researchers also noted that high relational trust is not necessarily built during special retreats, workshops or meetings but rather is woven into the day-to-day routines and life of the school. What the Chicago research and our Canadian case study research have shown is that trust is not simply a desirable quality; trust is essential for learning improvement for at least four reasons.

Making important changes to practice at the school level is often risky for the adults involved. Teachers and support staff may be asked to incorporate new practices that do not seem to fit well in their contexts nor suit their individual styles. Parents are sometimes expected to support initiatives before there is adequate local evidence of the positive value of the changes.

In a context of increasingly demanding and fast-paced reforms, leaders who have trusting relationships with parents and with staff can moderate and manage the stress and feelings of vulnerability that come from high levels of uncertainty. School leaders who build a trusting culture have the social capital to choose their directions wisely rather than simply conforming to external and often competing demands.

In most policy settings, there is pressure for changes to be made quickly. In 1995 Larry Cuban described the sense of time of the various reform clocks as being on media, policy maker or bureaucratic time – not on learner or teacher time – and reform time has been on fast-forward ever since. Today, schools across jurisdictions find the pace of policy announcements and programme initiatives to be relentless. Time pressures and an overwhelming sense of urgency, work against the desire for well-planned, thoughtful programme change.

Moving quickly and productively to implement new policy directions requires effective school-level decision-making. When trust levels are low, the transaction costs of the decisions are high. When there are high levels of earned trust, however, the discretionary scope of the formal and informal leaders in the school is much larger. Decisions can be made more readily and with greater collective understanding. Schools with high levels of trust are characterized by staff clarity on role obligations. By demonstrating their reliability in day-to-day actions, staff members develop the expectation that productive work by every individual is the norm. This creates an environment in which a highly directive, supervisory approach is much less often or seldom required.

In schools where relationships of trust have not been developed, leaders sometimes make the mistake of using 'top-down' decisions regarding professional development and 'inspection' of classroom practices as ways of speeding up the pace of school improvement. These strategies seldom have the desired outcomes. In schools where the leaders take the time required to build trust with parents and staff and demonstrate through their thoughtful decisions and transparent organization practices that they are competent in key areas of school life, the momentum for positive change is slowly and steadily increased. In schools with intense moral purpose, the adults – staff and parents – demonstrate a strong moral obligation to work together for the benefit of their young people. Participants agree to place the needs of the learners above their own individual interests. High levels of relational trust help to reinforce the moral purpose of the school and are reflected in the ethical behaviour of the adults associated with the school. As well, it can be argued that the work of building trusting relationships is critical to developing a civic and democratic school life.

The importance of trusting relationships in transforming learning for young people is connected with the ideas of Robert Putnam (2000) and his views on social capital. He points out that the effective working of all democratic institutions rests on the willingness of citizens to work collectively together on matters of mutual concern. For civic engagement to work, strong social ties and high levels of interpersonal trust at the community level are required.

Most educators intuitively understand that they are operating in a community where social capital and the trust it brings to the learning enterprise are critical. Many educators also believe that developing trusting relationships based on respect and positive regard is increasingly important in our multicultural communities and global world. They understand the importance of developing the tough (as opposed to 'soft') interpersonal and citizenship skills required for learners of all ages. Relational trust is fundamental to strong learning cultures and has a positive impact on learning outcomes. But where does a new leader start? How does a school leader determined to shift the school to a stronger learning orientation develop trust during the day-to-day interactions – with individuals, departments or with the faculty as a whole?

Developing relational trust

Chris wanted to let people know that he was serious about improving student learning – and that he could be trusted. He worked hard to get to know the staff personally and individually. He was determined to learn the names of all of the students and parents – at least as many as he could. He found out about the talents and interests of the students and what interested them about their learning. He resisted doing email or paperwork during the school day and was conscious about the importance of every interaction with staff, parents and students – whether in the hallway, parking lot, classroom, or staff room – as an opportunity to express his interest in student learning.

Chris had individual conversations with each teacher during the first month of school and during these conversations he asked them to tell him about two students they felt were doing very well in their classes – and why. Next he asked them to tell him about two students who were struggling and what they could do as a school team to help those learners. Finally he asked them to tell him about the students who could easily be missed in class because they didn't stand out as either excelling or as struggling. He listened carefully and made a point of connecting with these specific learners during his regular classroom visits.

Chris was also aware that many of the parents of students new to the country did not attend the first parent evening, nor were they represented on the parent council. He contacted the immigrant services society, arranged for a translator to invite parents individually and set up a series of 'coffee sessions' at the local community centre. Inviting a teacher or two with him each time, he listened attentively to the stories of hardship experienced by many of the families who had sacrificed a great deal to provide their children with a better life and a good education in their new country. He listened to their hopes and dreams for their children; he listened to their apprehensions about coming to the school. He asked for their suggestions about how to make the school a more welcoming place for new families – and he started to integrate their suggestions into observable actions.

Bryk and Schneider (2002) argue that:

> As social interactions occur, individuals attend simultaneously to the behavior of others (that is, the outcomes occurring and the observable processes being deployed to advance those outcomes), to how they personally feel about these interactions and to their beliefs about the underlying intentions that motivate all of this.
>
> (p. 21)

As parents and teachers observe the behaviour of the new formal leader, they make judgments as to the leader's intentions. Teachers and parents who have a reason to believe that changes being championed by the principal have more to do with personal career enhancement than what is good for the learners and their families will be slow to offer trust. Parents who have had difficult experiences themselves as learners in school, or who feel that they have not been listened to by formal leaders in the past, will be duly cautious in letting themselves believe in the new principal. As these adults watch the principal, they will be wondering: Is she sincere? Is he being respectful to our community and to our past? Is she following through on what she said she would do? Do his actions match his words? Is she capable of making the 'right' decisions even though they may be tough? Does she know who I am? Does he care?

The good news is that trust can be built. The bad news is that trust can be easily eroded – and once gone, trust is difficult to restore. Blasé and Blasé (2003) have documented a considerable number of ways that school leaders can have a negative effect on the trust levels of the staffs with which they work. Harmful leaders ignore or discount the feelings of their teachers, criticize teachers unfairly and give inaccurate and unfair performance appraisals. Examining the effect of poor leadership in the spheres of politics and business, Kellerman (2004) describes the negative effects of seven forms of bad leadership. Her descriptions of poor leaders with issues of rigidity, incompetence or insularity are lenses that can be used to examine poor school leadership as well. In an examination of the impact of toxic leadership in work and political settings Lipman-Blumen (2005) describes the importance of leaders avoiding negative competition and ego-driven motivation and she urges followers to find the inner strength to reject leaders and styles that limit autonomy and inclusivity.

Many of the new and experienced school leaders we work with have a trust mindset; they are aware of the importance of avoiding negative forms of leadership (often from their own prior experiences) and understand the importance of *every* interaction from their first moment associated with the school. Parents, teachers and support staff will develop trust in their school leader if they see evidence of the following four dimensions: respect, personal regard, integrity and competence in core responsibilities.

Respect

Chris had been warned by his predecessor about the attitude of some of the experienced teachers on the staff. Resistant, cynical and negative were words he had heard used to describe some of his new colleagues. Chris felt it was possible that the teachers had been damaged by the actions of leaders in the past and he knew he needed to build trust carefully. He created every possible opportunity to be with teachers on their own turf – whether in the gym, the music room, or the classroom – and at a time that worked for them. He knew who the early birds were and he knew who had to leave school promptly to pick up their children. He encouraged them to talk about the strategies they were finding most useful in engaging their learners and their hopes for the school. He listened deeply.

'Communication trust' is one of the forms of trust described by Reina and Reina (1999) in *Trust and Betrayal in the Workplace*. They argue that communication trust is evident in human interactions that convey shared understanding and good intentions. Bryk and Schneider (2002) suggest that:

> Respect involves recognition of the important role each person plays in a child's education and the mutual dependencies that

exist among various parties involved in this activity. Key in this regard is how conversation takes place within a school community. .

(p. 23)

Active listening is one of the first requirements of effective dialogue. It is a key skill in building trust and is not easy to do. As Jan Robertson (2005) says, 'to listen for even three or four minutes without interrupting and without sharing one's own stories or giving advice is something that leaders often find difficult' (p. 110). Overcoming the impulse to give advice and to solve teacher problems, sometimes before genuinely understanding the problem context, are important aspects of growth for a leader who is motivated to build trusting relationships with her adult colleagues. Often teachers are not looking to the leader to offer a solution. What they want is to be heard, to be understood and then to feel supported in finding their own solution.

In the positive school communities we have observed, respect is generally based on the belief of all individuals that they are being deeply listened to and understood, rather than just being heard. Teachers in these schools report that their principal values the diversity of style and the differing points of view of the adults in the building. As these school leaders seek out and then listen actively to a range of voices – parents, teachers, support staff, students – genuine dialogue occurs and this creates the potential for the kind of communication that will move the school community forward in its learning orientation.

Rosabeth Moss-Kanter in her book (2004), *Confidence: How Winning and Losing Streaks Begin and End,* notes:

> If people look positively at themselves and the hidden value of their assets, they are more likely to discover strengths that they can cultivate. If people look positively at others, those people are more likely to come through for them. And if people look positively at the opportunities any situation provides to take even a small step, they are more likely to find that their actions make a difference.

(p. 368)

Creating a confidence-building culture is important and challenging work. Restoring trust in cultures that have been damaged by lack of trust is an arduous process that requires humility, patience and effort. A rapid turnover of formal school leaders coupled with the intensification of expectations and accountability demands from policy-makers can increase teacher cynicism and skepticism. Tschannen-Moran (2004) suggests: 'trust repair is facilitated by working for good communication, being meticulously reliable and using persuasion rather than coercion' (p. 161). Restoring trust is not easy work. As anyone who has tried to repair a damaged relationship knows, it takes time, persistence and resilience. For leaders dealing with multiple individuals, the work is complex, demanding and challenging. Every single interaction provides another opportunity to either build or erode trust. Deep, careful listening and displaying personal regard for every individual are crucial in this process.

Personal regard

As Chris reviewed the student learning evidence from the final examinations held over the past few years, he noticed an anomaly. The results, both in participation and success rates, from Birgit, one of the English teachers, seemed to be significantly stronger year after year than other members of her department. When Chris asked her what she thought contributed to her success, she seemed genuinely perplexed. She knew she had good content knowledge and instructional skills – but so did her colleagues. She said that Sanjai, a new school counsellor, had asked the same question. Chris suggested that perhaps the two of them would like to engage in a small action research project to explore this question. Over the next few months, Chris provided release time for Birgit and Sanjai to engage in peer observation and to hold conversations with parents and students.

What emerged from their exploration was deceptively simple. Every day, Birgit spent a few moments with every one of her students talking to them about something other than English. She knew what teams they were on, what interests they had and what was happening with their families. When they missed class, she phoned them personally. When they had a success, she was there to cheer them on. Her students felt she genuinely cared about them and they would do anything they could to show her they were worthy of her trust. As a result, even the learners with especially challenging life circumstances never missed her classes. As a result of Sanjai's interest in her work, Birgit was able to bring her tacit practices to a conscious level of understanding. Chris knew he could learn a lot from Birgit about connecting with his staff.

Bryk and Schneider (2002) observed that trust grows as individuals 'go the extra mile' to show caring. 'In general, interpersonal trust deepens as individuals perceive that others care about them and are willing to extend themselves beyond what their role might formally require in any given situation' (p. 25). By reducing the sense of vulnerability of others, interpersonal trust is enhanced. School leaders promote trust by showing consideration and sensitivity for staff members' individual needs and interests. Principals demonstrate caring and build trust when they know and understand the challenges that staff members may be facing in their personal lives. Who is dealing with an aging parent? Whose child is sick? Who is in the process of moving house? Whose partner has just lost a job? Further, principals also show personal regard when they create opportunities for teachers' career development. Who has just started a masters' programme? Who is interested in expanding their sphere of influence? Who is hoping to assume more formal leadership responsibilities? Who would like to become qualified in a new subject area?

Bryk and Schneider's (2002, 2003) work also emphasizes the importance of developing relational trust with parents. Many parents and families we have worked with dread getting a phone call or an email from the school since in their experience this usually means a problem. In contrast, we have observed the positive impact that occurs when teachers or principals take the time at the end of the day to call parents with a short positive piece of information about a learner. Many leaders we know find that doing this regularly on a Friday afternoon has the biggest impact. Why Friday? Most families have a bit more time together on the weekend and the chances are better that the 'good news story' will be shared repeatedly to the learner's benefit.

Teachers and parents, who are carrying a legacy of misplaced trust in previous leaders, are often justifiably slow to warm to the efforts of the new leader. Fear, doubt and anxiety can be manifested as cynicism and indifference. Bryk and Schneider (2002, 2003) indicated that to build relational trust, the individuals with the most power have to make themselves vulnerable to the others. By genuinely sharing our own concerns and worries as leaders, we can help others to see us as human beings with human frailties. Taking the step of asking for advice, seeking out opinions and sharing our personal stories creates a sense of mutuality and connection. Parents state that they want to know their teachers and principals as human beings first and as professionals second. Leaders who let themselves be known as parents, as family members, as people with interests and hobbies and as individuals with dreams and apprehensions are making important strides in building trust. Despite all best efforts, however, the road to trust building is rarely smooth, as we will see next with Chris.

Personal integrity

Chris believed that one way to break down the isolation among teachers, to create a greater sense of teamwork and to show them that he was serious about learning, was to provide regular communication about what he was seeing in his classroom visits. So from the first week of school he sent out a weekly bulletin acknowledging individual teachers for the learning work he had observed. 'You might be interested in asking Lisa about the ways she is using the "no hands" strategy to build individual responsibility in her Math classes.' 'Raj's use of the imaginative strategies of binary opposites and metaphor really seems to be building engagement in Social Studies. I found it hard to leave the lesson.' Each week he was careful to include a range of teachers and subject areas and to be descriptive rather than judgemental in his comments. He thought he was on the right track.

One Monday in mid-October he went to the staff room for an early morning coffee. There on the wall was a large poster with the names of every staff member and the date when they had been acknowledged in one of Chris's bulletins. The heading for the poster was 'Principal's suck hole list.' He felt like he had been punched in the stomach.

After taking some time to think it through, Chris decided that this act was presenting him with a challenge to see whether or not he was 'for real'. He decided to stay with his practice. Week after week, he persisted in sharing insights and observations about the strong learning work he was seeing. Week after week, the poster was updated. One day in February, the poster came down. No one said a word.

Integrity is reflected when there is a match between words and actions. In schools, parents, teachers and students watch the formal leader very carefully to see if there is consistency between what is said and what is done. Does the leader 'walk the talk'? Can the principal be trusted to keep his word? Will she stick to her espoused beliefs when things get tough? When trust has been eroded or betrayed, individuals look for ways to protect themselves from further hurt. Canadian professional learning community researchers Mitchell and Sackney (2000) note:

> Trust is a critical factor in bringing about profound improvement in a school. Without trust, people divert their energy into self-protection and away from learning. Where trust is lacking, people will not take the risks necessary to move the school forward.
>
> (p. 49)

In negative cultures staff energy can go into consciously or unconsciously creating 'tests' to see whether the leader is genuine. Leaders with a trust mindset understand that scars from previous relationships can take a long time to heal and they hold the belief that healing can and will take place. Leaders with intense moral purpose – and a trust mindset – will find the strength to persevere even when there are apparent setbacks. If the principal says she values the learning of every young person in the building and through her actions she shows this to be true, then teachers and parents will begin to develop trust. Knowing and using pupil names, especially in large secondary schools, is a measure of respect. Knowing the learning interests and needs of the learners is next. Communicating frequently and personally with families follows.

One of the simplest strategies we have seen in this regard involves principals, regardless of the size or level of the school, personally providing specific feedback and encouragement on each learner's report card. This is a relatively common practice in elementary schools, but less so in secondary schools. Although time consuming, the impact of this form of personalized communication cannot be underestimated. The specific descriptive nature of the feedback lets learners and parents know that the formal leaders not only know and care about each individual, but that they also expect them to use the feedback to improve their learning. The key here is consistency. Once leaders make the commitment to provide individual feedback, they must stick with it or their integrity will be questioned and trust eroded.

Leaders who demonstrate respect through deep listening, build personal regard through caring for individuals and the community and have high degrees of personal integrity are well equipped to build – or rebuild – trust. If, however, the leader does not pay attention to specific job related expectations, trust will not develop. In other words, it is not enough to be a good person; a leader must also be good at the work of school leadership.

Competence

Shortly after Chris arrived at Riverbank he became aware of the 'trouble spots' in the school. Student discipline was inconsistent and reactive. Lunch hour was marked by tension; fights were common; hallway conversations were peppered with swearing and put-downs; teachers had withdrawn to their classrooms or the staff room; parents were worried about safety and concerned about bullying. Creating an orderly, respectful tone was a priority.

Chris was everywhere about the building during period breaks, before school, after school, at noon hour. He shared his concerns about tone and behaviour with the staff, student leadership groups and parents. He asked for their help. A staff-student group started to research positive discipline programmes and approaches. They reported their findings at staff meetings. He arranged a series of staff-student focus groups to develop common expectations and students were taught what was expected through classroom meetings and grade assemblies – and Chris showed what he expected through his constant presence.

It is not surprising to anyone who has worked in a school that competence in core responsibilities is identified by researchers as one of the key components of trust (Tschannen-Moran and Hoy 1998; Bryk and Schneider 2003; Tschannen-Moran 2004). What is interesting, however, is that the criteria for competence can vary widely in each school setting:

> Interestingly, applications of the competence criterion in school settings often involve significant asymmetry. Judgments about high standards of performance are hard to validate ... The fundamental character of schooling – its multiple aims, the complex mechanisms needed to advance them and the lack of good data on actual practice – makes it exceedingly difficult to answer such questions as: Is a principal really exemplary at leading school improvement? Is a teacher employing best practice in reading instruction? Are parents doing all they can to support schoolwork at home?
>
> (Bryk and Schneider 2003, p. 24)

The difficulties that the researchers describe do not prevent us as educators and parents from making judgments about school leaders. Agreement around clear criteria for high levels of competence may vary, but we have found broad general agreement about incompetence. Judgments about incompetence of principals arise, for example, when parents observe a school where the language of the young people is disrespectful and the environment is disorderly or where some teachers hold low expectations for the behaviour and achievement of their learners. Parents, students and fellow teachers are often all too aware of struggling teachers and watch with great interest to see what a new leader will do to address the negative learning situation. As Viviane Robinson (2007) notes:

> Allowed to persist, gross incompetence is highly corrosive to trust and undermines collective efforts at school improvement. This may help explain why teachers' perceptions of their principal's ability to identify and deal effectively with conflict were strongly related to student achievement. Leaders who are conflict avoiders or conflict escalators will be unlikely to deal with competence issues in a timely and effective manner. When conditions of disorder and disrespect persist over time, trust is eroded.
>
> (p. 19)

When leaders demonstrate a willingness to deal with conflict and to address problematic issues, trust builds – and when trust builds, learners benefit. Sometimes building trust requires a change in routines and often long-held rituals. Here's an example from Riverbank:

One of the inherited structures at Riverbank was a parent-teacher evening at the end of the first month of school. No one was happy with this evening. Many of the teachers had referred to the previous year's event as 'Meet the Creature' and had refused to show up – they went to the pub instead. This was mortifying for the previous leader and Chris knew things had to change. Parents wanted to meet the teachers, but a whirlwind of 'sit and git' information sessions did not meet their needs for connecting with individual staff members. Chris raised the possibility with the school chef of replacing the parent-teacher evening with a family barbecue where staff, learners and parents would all be invited. The staff expressed a willingness to try a different approach and the barbecue was well attended by families and by staff. The change in routine was considered by all involved to represent a positive beginning in shifting relationships and creating a greater sense of respect and community.

Based on her close observations of leadership trust-building activities in three schools with varying degrees of relational trust, Kochanek (2005) proposed the following guidelines for leaders to consider:

> Schools starting with a low base state of trust must spend more time on mechanisms that set the stage for trust and promote successful, low risk interactions, rather than on those that promote more high-risk interactions. Therefore, school professionals in low-trust environments must invest more effort into mechanisms that ease vulnerabilities, such as social activities; easily accomplished projects; communication of a common vision; small-group meetings; and positive, daily interactions.
>
> (p. 73)

To understand the evidence-informed suggestions for practice she makes, it is important to consider more closely the role of vulnerability reduction in the trust-building process. Trust has been likened to the 'oil' that allows communication and work to move forward smoothly. Bryk and Schneider (2003) found evidence in their school studies that there is a mutual vulnerability of parents, staff and principals that is often unacknowledged.

New leaders in a school can appreciate the research evidence that principals feel and are vulnerable to the goodwill and collective effort of teachers. This is particularly true when changes to benefit learners are urgently required. Teachers feel vulnerable to the views and behaviours of parents and of their principal. Parents, especially those who live in conditions of poverty, feel vulnerable to the opinions of teachers and the principal. Bryk and Schneider (2002) concluded: 'the key operational feature of a school community is not its power distribution, but rather a set of mutual dependencies and, with them, mutual vulnerability' (p. 183). They note that the redistribution of power does not by itself address the concern that in order to improve student learning, informal and formal leaders must recognize mutual dependencies among parties. Changing the distribution of power 'may change the specific representation of the dependency and vulnerability in an organization, but it does not eliminate their consideration' (p. 183).

Another useful insight from this study was that, in the trust building process, the individual or group with the most power had to express vulnerability first. Power is not necessarily equated with a formal role. Sometimes a small group of teachers have the power to exert a great deal of influence on their colleagues. Sometimes a parent group believes and acts as if it has the ultimate authority and sometimes it is the formal leader whose authority dominates. By expressing vulnerability, a foundation for trust building can be created. We have found that when teachers, principals and parents can talk together about their feelings of mutual vulnerability and when they come to understand that power relationships are not fixed but shift depending on the situation, the notion of the person with the most power having to make themselves vulnerable first makes a lot of sense.

Chris breathed a small sigh of relief. June had arrived and with it the end of his first year at Riverbank. He had just concluded a conversation with two Math teachers, Blake and Lisa. Despite two satisfactory teaching reports over the past 20 years, Blake was struggling – and so were his learners. Success rates in his classes were low and frustration was high. Lisa was a skilled teacher and a keen learner. She had had many conversations with Chris during the year about her recent graduate work and how she was building learner engagement and success through formative assessment. Chris had also spent a lot of time during the year with Blake – developing rapport, sharing his concerns and discussing strategies to improve learning and build trust with his students. Ignoring the situation in Blake's classes was simply 'not on'. Chris hoped that Lisa might be willing to accept the challenge of sharing her enthusiasm and expertise with Blake and Chris had met several times with them to discuss possibilities for teaming the following year.

The purpose of this final year-end meeting was to confirm that Lisa and Blake would engage in a shared inquiry as learning partners with two Year 10 Math classes when school resumed. During the summer the three of them were going to attend an institute on formative assessment and Chris would make sure that Lisa and Blake had adequate time to plan for the classes they would share. Despite being somewhat nervous, Lisa was excited about the opportunity to work with Blake and Chris. This would give her a chance to help a colleague and to develop her own leadership skills. And, although apprehensive, Blake was willing to give it a go. He knew he had to make some changes and he knew that Chris was trying to give him a chance to improve as a teacher.

The meeting ended with both Blake and Lisa expressing cautious optimism about their teamwork plans. Chris sensed they appreciated his belief in their ability to work together to improve Math learning. He believed it was important that he would be learning with them and that he would be asking for their feedback as he worked to make staff meetings more engaging and purposeful. Blake, Lisa and Chris were each making themselves vulnerable.

Conclusion

Competence in core responsibilities for leaders with a trust mindset clearly means more than just ensuring the smooth management of the school. It does mean confronting the situations in which learner needs are not being fully served. We have seen formal leaders who have worked hard to demonstrate respect, who show caring through demonstrating personal regard and who are often described as 'very nice' people – but who have failed in their responsibility to tackle the truly difficult situations. Ultimately trust is eroded if parents, young people and staff members do not believe they can count on the formal leader to intervene on behalf of learners and quality learning. School leaders, formal and informal, who have a mindset of intense moral purpose, who put learning and learners at the centre of their work and who appreciate the importance of all aspects of trust building, do not shy away from the tough calls.

Mindsets of intense moral purpose and trust are key to establishing a clear sense of purpose and to building relationships. Without intense moral purpose, schools and their leaders can all too easily accept the status quo. Without trusting relationships, the chances of a school making the shift from sorting to learning are remote. In the next chapter, we will explore the inquiry mindset and the importance of approaching school improvement through inquiry rather than through an attitude of premature certainty.

Questions for consideration

1   You have just moved to a school where the culture is one of mistrust. As a principal or teacher leader, what will be your first steps in developing positive relationships with your colleagues, your learners and their families?

2   As a principal, clearly communicating that every decision you make will be based on what you believe to be the best for learners – as individuals and as a group – is important. How will you do this? How will you ensure that your actions match your words?

3   Working together on small, easily accomplished projects is one of the identified strategies in building trust. Shared work allows for a sense of success and provides an initial experience of mutual respect and regard. For Chris, the family barbecue provided a small start. Team learning and joint inquiry with Blake and Lisa

also helped. What kind of project would make sense in your context?

4   Small meetings of staff members, students and families with a single focus allow for lively discussion and active participation. Chris was able to get staff and students involved in small committees to generate suggestions and strategies related to student discipline and school tone. The energy of the small group was used to communicate the ideas to larger groups of students, families and staff. Feedback was sought and used. This strategy, consistently applied over time created a new culture of trust and mutual respect. What is the focus for improvement in your school? How will you structure opportunities for small focused meetings? How will you demonstrate respect, personal regard, integrity and competence in the way you organize for improvement?

5   Sometimes we have seen leaders who do not take advantage of the opportunities presented by the multiple interactions in which they are involved on a daily basis. Of these principals, staff members say with a sigh: 'I'm glad I'm not a principal. She is always so busy. Her door is always shut or she is away at meetings.' What message will you convey about your values through your use of time? Are you embracing or avoiding inter-actions? How are you using the many interactions you have – or can have – during the day to build trust? To focus on learning?

6   When a trusting culture exists, leaders can use this resource to build an even stronger set of results for learners. Keeping in mind the wry observation about the impact of learning improvements being in inverse proportion to the length of the written school improvement plan, how can you use the trust that you have developed to move learning forward in a conscious, planned and compelling way?

Chapter 4

Inquiry – questions before directions

Leaders with an inquiry habit of mind do not presume an outcome; instead they allow for a range of outcomes and keep searching for increased understanding and clarity. Inquiry-mindedness demands engagement in questioning, reflecting and decision-making (p. 9).

Collaborative inquiry merges deep collaboration in the form of rigorous and challenging joint work with inquiry and is consistent with Little's (2005) reference to a large body of research suggesting that conditions for improving learning and teaching are strengthened when teachers collectively question ineffective teaching routines, examine new conceptions of teaching and learning, find generative means to acknowledge and respond to difference and conflict and engage actively in supporting one another's professional growth (p. 124).

Educators may not be experienced or comfortable with these inquiry processes of questioning, reflecting, seeking alternatives and weighing consequences to promote the 'transparency' of what might remain unobservable facets of practice, making tacit knowledge visible and open to scrutiny (p. 124).

Lorna Earl and Helen Timperley (2008)
Professional Learning Conversations:
Challenges in Using Evidence for Improvement

Cathy Sakai was on her way to her first staff meeting at the school where she had just been appointed principal. New job, new school and new district – she was nervous, excited and eager to get to work. She had carefully studied the school growth plan and noted that literacy had been the focus for several years. She hadn't been able to find much evidence from the school plan that results were improving and she believed that her strong background as a literacy helping teacher would be a real asset. As she walked from the parking lot, she noticed the litter blowing around the entrance, the dilapidated picnic tables and the large sign instructing visitors to report directly to the office.

Inside, she saw a faded notice advising parents about the treatment for head lice and an announcement about an upcoming retirement seminar. The secretary looked up briefly from her computer to tell her that the staff were waiting for her in the library – and cautioned her that the staff were disappointed that the former principal had been transferred against his will. As she made her way to the library, Cathy decided to keep an open mind and to ask lots of questions – before leaping in with her literacy plans.

In our work with schools in varied contexts, we have found that the strongest school leaders are characterized by constant curiosity and a mindset of persistent inquiry. In his studies of leaders who work in complex multicultural contexts, researcher Allan Walker (2006) noted the key role of inquiry mindedness, which he describes as curiosity, in expanding options for improvement action:

> Curious leaders maintain an open mind; actively wonder about things; ask lots of questions; and show interest in the possibility that things are not always as they seem at first glance. Curiosity is also about reframing, or the capacity to see things in new ways – ways that generate fresh options for leadership action and for learning.
>
> (p. 19)

The inquiry-minded leaders with whom we work believe that there is always more to learn that would be useful to the adults and to the young learners in their schools. Inquiry-minded leaders avoid the complacency or cynicism that sometimes comes with experience – the 'been there, done that before' stance of their less effective colleagues.

In highly directive policy contexts, inquiry-mindedness also acts as an antidote to mindless compliance. Studies of leaders in two North American settings (Hargreaves and Fink 2006; Mertz and McNeely 1998) found that leaders who were able to realize the greatest long term learning gains for both staff and students, consciously utilized the energy of state and district directives. These leaders built on and 'used' the mandates to inquire productively into the long-term benefits and tradeoffs of the new directions. They then worked in unique and sustained ways to maximize learning benefits. Their less effective colleagues often moved too quickly and obediently to respond to policy directions, occasionally got faster gains in test scores, but then were unable to deepen learning or create further improvements.

Simply applying strategies that promise 'guaranteed' solutions is not enough for thoughtful leaders. Ann Lieberman (2004) and her colleagues who have studied sustained networks of improving schools in the United States suggest that:

> An inquiry stance is far different from a solution stance. It requires that one ask questions of one's practice rather than look for answers. It places contextual data collection and analysis rather than generalized solutions at the centre of improvement efforts.
>
> (p. 41)

Emily Calhoun and Bruce Joyce (2005) also make the case for an inquiry mindset, based on their research evidence regarding the perceived failures of the two major strategies for school improvement used in many jurisdictions around the world: the classic, external research and professional development approach and the school-based, faculty-centred approach:

> We believe that the advocates of both the major paradigms made essentially the same reasonable mistake: *they believed they had a sure fire strategy, that they were unlikely to fail and thus, didn't conduct school improvement as an inquiry, making modifications as they went.*
>
> (p. 262; italics in original)

They conclude that it would be a serious mistake to discard either set of strategies and urge instead a much more inquiry-oriented approach that combines the best of both strategies and relies on careful thinking, planning, support and reflection in action.

In our case studies of school change, we have found that those schools that are led by educators with an inquiry habit of mind have the greatest impact on improving deep learning for understanding over time. These leaders understand and know when and how to apply at least four forms of inquiry in strategic and appropriate ways. They bring insights from the traditions of narrative, appreciative, critical/problem-based and reflective inquiry to their work. In this chapter we provide a brief description of each form of inquiry and we will follow Cathy as she applies the various forms of inquiry to transform learning in her school.

Narrative inquiry

*In her first few weeks, as Cathy visited teachers in their classrooms, sat in on meetings, shared coffee in the staff room, chatted with children on the play-ground and met with parents in the parking lot, she heard stories of sadness, discouragement and lack of trust. 'This used to be a good school – now look at it! No one from the board office even knows we exist.' 'Mr Jones was such a great teacher. I wish he was still here.' 'My son is being picked on and no one seems to care.' 'Remember the play we put on a few years ago? Now that was terrific!' 'The Year Sevens are all mean to us.' 'We are collecting data that no one understands or uses – just because **they** say we have to.' I don't know why my pupils aren't reading better. I am teaching the same way I always have and they simply don't get it.' 'Why don't the parents send their kids better prepared? Don't they care?' 'I always wonder what teachers do on those professional days. It's a bit of a mystery.'*

One of the fundamental assumptions of narrative inquiry is that human beings and stories are intertwined – that stories are the foun-dation of our identity. The narrative researcher Molly Andrews (2000) suggests that:

> Stories are not only the way in which we come to ascribe signifi-cance to experiences but also they are one of the primary means through which we constitute our very selves. We become who we are through telling stories about our lives and living the stories we tell.
>
> (p. 77)

When a leader goes to their new school for the first time, one of the strategic approaches from the inquiry repertoire is that of discover-ing the dominant stories that the staff, student and community members tell about the school. Who are the heroes? Who are the villains? What are the successes? What are the challenges? What are the defining moments in the school's history? What are the stories repeated at social events? At meetings? In professional dialogues? In living rooms? In coffee shops? In the early days in a new school, narrative inquiry can be especially useful to the leader as he or she listens to understand the culture of the school. The stories that are told about the school can reveal a great deal – especially if one also listens closely to the subtext.

School leaders may not necessarily use the pure, theoretical perspectives from the narrative inquiry literature (Clandinin and Connelly 2000, p. 16). They do, however, put the practices to work tacitly or consciously by drawing on the traditions of description – how the staff use events in sequence as 'stories' to make their own lives and the life of the school meaningful, and explanation – accounting for the connection between events in a causal way.

A special strength of narrative inquiry, especially in a climate of high test-driven accountability, is that it can add a richness and humanity to the description of a school. In many places the impoverished description of a school told with a numbers-only perspective can be part of the negative self-concept of the school: 'We're the school at the bottom of the heap.' 'Our reading scores stink.' 'Teachers leave here as soon as they can.' Respectful deep listening, combined with thoughtful storytelling about new possibilities, can help teachers and community members explore what Andy Hargreaves (2002) described as the 'emotional geographies' of staff perspectives and in doing so, begin to provide an increasingly open space for new, more positive stories to emerge.

In our studies we have seen inquiry-minded leaders effectively using narrative inquiry and the pattern finding that is part of the discipline to begin to understand the setting, central characters, emotional tone, plot line and themes of their new schools. As leaders listen deeply to the stories of staff members, students and parents, they create hypotheses about the culture and begin to see patterns that help them to understand the current view of 'reality'. They also begin to shape the culture of the school by thinking about what stories they will tell.

In jurisdictions where schools often feel battered by media attention and league tables, researchers and practitioners alike are looking for new ways to strengthen school culture and to create genuine learning improvement. Inquiry-minded leaders start to think early on about the kind of stories they themselves can tell to shift the culture in a new direction. Where the school story has been one of discouragement and depression, we have seen inquiring leaders create new stories through effectively applying appreciative inquiry as an approach to their work in setting new directions and creating more positive cultures. Let's see how Cathy used appreciative inquiry to uncover and build on the strengths of the school.

Appreciative inquiry

In her early conversations with teachers, Cathy asked them: 'Think back to a time at school that you recall as a high point – an experience or moment that left you with an intense sense of pride, excitement or connection in having been part of something that was meaningful, a time that you really felt you had contributed to improving learning for an individual or a group.' She asked them to describe the experience in detail and she listened carefully to understand every nuance.

She regularly asked staff, parents and students what they were most proud of about the school – and she used every opportunity to reinforce the very real strengths that she observed. She asked teachers to tell her about one small thing they were doing that they were confident was helping to deepen learning. Cathy asked everyone to tell her about the successes they were having – and to identify what they believed were the root causes of these successes. She asked them to tell her about the things they wanted to keep doing – or to do even better – no matter what else changed. She asked them to say how they would like the school to be described in a year or two – and what role they might play in making that a reality.

Appreciative inquiry is a strengths-based, capacity building approach to changing human systems through developing a shared image of potential by first discovering the best in shared experiences. Proponents of appreciative inquiry (Barrett and Fry 2005) believe that it is:

- systems-oriented rather than fragmented;
- possibility driven rather than past focused;
- oriented to positive discourse rather than engaged with deficit prophesies;
- actively oriented towards knowledge of the school participants and away from an over-reliance on hierarchy and external experts;
- concerned with the development of positive rather than stressful, negative emotions; and
- intensely interested in replacing spirals of separation with a holistic view of the school (pp. 30–1).

Many school leaders find that the use of appreciative inquiry as a form of investigation, infuses renewed energy into their school community. These leaders use an affirmative question to help others in the school acquire new habits of mind. They demonstrate what Barrett and Fry indicate a number of not-for-profit and business leaders understand – that one of the characteristics of great organizations is that 'they ask the right questions *and* they pay attention to the results even if the answers imply the need for simple or radical changes' (2005, p. 10). They go on to note 'learning always begins with a question, a moment of inquiry. These questions represent attempts to learn that often result in efforts to improve performance, or to better a situation in some ways' (2005, p. 15).

Appreciative inquiry uses a four-stage set of processes – of discovering, dreaming, designing and destiny – to create pictures of transformational change possibility. Figure 4.1, adapted from the work of Barratt and Fry, illustrates what this process can look like when it is applied to learning-focused schools. Supporters of appreciative inquiry claim that school leaders lower stress and create positive momentum by working with their staff and communities to discover strengths, to imagine possible futures, to design new ways forward and to create a different future by taking on action research projects in a highly inclusive manner.

Appreciative inquiry has been applied in a variety of settings and has been found to be an effective strategy in generating creative momentum for organizations that are stuck. Alan Daly and Janet Chrispeels (2005) have been studying the application of the ideas of appreciative inquiry and positive psychology to school and district

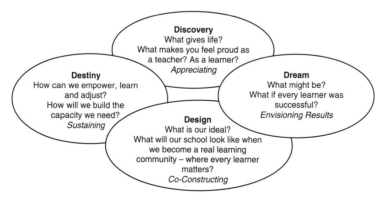

Figure 4.1 Appreciative inquiry cycle.

improvement. They argue that a new approach to improving schools should be used in light of the stress created by demands for higher system performance, narrow accountability measures, league tables and intense media coverage of system failures. They suggest that the negative impact of these stresses on schools serving the neediest communities are even greater because of the absence of the development and use of value-added measures. The absence of the use of these fairer measures of learning almost always leaves these schools at the bottom of public rankings. Daly and Chrispeels (2005) believe that school improvement can be enhanced by appreciating individual school strengths and by actively searching for positive deviance improvements on which to build. They note:

> This radical paradigm shift will not be easy and will require schools, universities and consultants to be intentional about their focus on the possible and to empower educational leaders from all parts of the system to renew their commitments to strengths based approaches. Leaders will need to facilitate processes that examine the root causes of success that build the efficacy of all in the systems and create cultures of hope and limitless potential. Students deserve and await a strengths-based environment in every school.
>
> (p. 20)

David Cooperrider (2001), a key proponent of appreciative inquiry, maintains that most organizations, products and new services start first as wild but not idle dreams and he believes that positive images of possibility drive creative change. We have seen school leaders use the power of appreciative inquiry to create new learning cultures for adults and young people in places that, previous to their arrival, were stuck and stagnant. These leaders work 'as if' a new story is being formed. They actively create new meaning for the people with whom they work.

Narrative inquiry appeals to the storyteller in all of us. It helps us makes sense of our world and our work. Appreciative inquiry helps create pictures of possibility and helps to develop a stronger sense of collective worth. Both these approaches are important but we have found that they are not sufficient for a leader with a genuine inquiry mindset. Learning-oriented leaders probe into and confront the issues that are keeping the school from moving forward. They want to know what is getting in the way of maximizing learning for every learner. They are concerned about the young people who are not currently enjoying success and they want to understand why this is the case. School leaders determined to improve learning quality extend the contribution of narrative and appreciative forms of inquiry by applying problem-based, critical inquiry to their work.

Problem-based inquiry

Cathy worked hard to develop trusting relationships and to model respect, personal regard and integrity in every interaction with parents, learners, support staff and her teaching colleagues. She provided staff with carefully selected current articles and began sharing informally what she was learning in her Masters' programme. She was concerned that, despite the stated focus on improving reading comprehension, there was little discussion of the programmes or strategies that teachers were using. Reading practices varied widely class to class and she had observed that the learners could not identify the reading strategies they were using to understand their texts.

She was aware of the dissatisfaction expressed by staff about the standardized, technology based approach to reading assessment required by the district. Cathy had discussed these observations with Debbie, her leadership-coaching partner and she knew she had to open up the discussion about both reading and assessment at her school. She also knew that she needed to continue to build the kind of trust that would allow her to probe more deeply into professional practice. It was time to draw on her network of contacts.

She consulted with a knowledgeable reading consultant from outside her district and she shared her questions about assessment practices with two of her university professors. In partnership with a well-respected teacher colleague from another school, she invited staff to join a book club that they would host once a month. She was relieved and pleased when more than half the staff showed up to the first meeting. The group decided to focus on two books – one on reading strategies and one on formative assessment. Cathy was able to use the books, the coaching she had from her own network of contacts, and the objectivity of the teacher from the neighboring school to raise deeper questions about practice. Together the group started to probe some long held assumptions about the effectiveness of the reading programmes and approaches they were using.

In addition to the importance of surfacing the stories that form the identity of the school and the strengths, hopes and dreams of the school community, strong leaders also bring a critical inquiry lens to their learning improvement work. Two New Zealand researchers with a deep interest in educator action research, Viviane Robinson and Mai Kuin Lai (2006), have developed a problem-based methodology that relies heavily on critical inquiry as a means of improving learning. They insist that leaders must understand the theories of action that control classroom and school practice so that, as researching practitioners, they can both communicate their awareness of the learning and teaching challenges and be insightful about what and how, to improve. They suggest that improvement starts with describing, explaining and evaluating the current situation.

They note that in order to critically examine practice, a dialogue between two positions is required: teachers' *theories of action* (knowledge, beliefs and actions) and external researchers' *theoretical frameworks*. They observe that significant and worthwhile improvements to school and teacher practice require this constructive dialogue and they believe that this approach is much more powerful than simply providing academic research and theory to practitioners.

Experienced school leaders understand how difficult it is for teachers to be critical of the practice of another teacher. They also know that substantive professional growth will not occur unless there is an opportunity for genuine discussion and critique of theories of action. Robinson and Lai (2006) maintain that agreeing to an evaluative framework and establishing social and interpersonal processes up front can assist in overcoming the human tendency to avoid criticism. Their suggested framework for evaluating theories of action consists of four standards: accuracy, effectiveness, coherence and improvability (pp. 198–99).

Beginning with accuracy, the leader is curious about the extent to which what is claimed is actually happening in classrooms. Are school and department goals truly influencing teacher behaviour and learner experiences? For instance, are teachers actively developing and sharing success criteria with their learners? Can learners really articulate what it is they are supposed to be learning? Is there uninterrupted reading time in every classroom as indicated in the growth plan? Do learners have a repertoire of comprehension strategies? Are learners receiving the kind of descriptive feedback that will help them progress in their learning?

The second standard of effectiveness asks whether the theory of action as expressed in current practice delivers what was intended. Is ability-grouping for instruction actually helping to improve results without having a negative impact on learner motivation? Do parents find that the new reporting procedures are providing clearer information? Are learners more confident in understanding how they are being assessed? Is the work on cross-grade coaching in mathematical problem solving helping to increase the competence and confidence of both the older and younger learners?

The coherence criterion for evaluating theories of action considers the big picture. It asks whether the theory that teachers have used to solve a particular problem is compatible with high quality solutions to all the other problems for which they are responsible. The standard of coherence invites external 'critical friends' to provide additional perspectives regarding what the teachers themselves see as important. This standard creates the opportunity for challenges and changes to the insider views of teachers. It goes beyond the question of asking whether or not a theory of action delivers what practitioners themselves see as important. A critical friend might ask: 'How does your decision to deduct marks for late assignments match current knowledge about the impact of assessment practices on learning?' 'In what ways does the reading programme you have chosen help develop meta-cognition in your learners?' 'How has your cross-grade programme been informed by the initiatives currently underway in Scotland?' 'To what extent did the research on inclusion influence the development of your learning support programme?'

The use of the fourth standard, improvability, ensures that the solutions selected and the theories of action for moving forward are a good fit with the unique context and culture of the school. Improvability 'incorporates feedback loops that provide information about both intended and unintended consequences of actions so that beliefs about what works and why can be made explicit and checked' (Robinson and Lai, 2006, p. 31). Leaders with a focus on improvability understand that the approaches selected can be adapted to meet changing needs, new goals, shifting cultures and new policy contexts. Leaders with an inquiry mindset will always be checking to see how things are going, eliciting feedback in a range of ways and making adjustments as necessary. 'Let's try this for a semester and use each of our staff meetings to touch base on how things are going.' 'We're going to check regularly with each of you to see whether or not you need any additional support as we try this out.' 'We'll make sure that the district understands what we are doing and how our new approach to reading fits overall with the literacy focus.'

Problem-based inquiry and trust

In the previous chapter we saw how important relational trust is to improving learning. Positive connections and deep trust amongst the adults in a school are critical to school transformation work. Examining, exploring and confronting theories of action are also required for professional growth. School leaders who strive for deep professional learning understand that there will almost always be tensions when leaders and teachers engage in dialogue that is critical of some aspect of practice. Learning-oriented leaders recognize the simultaneous need for meaningful professional dialogue and trusting, respectful collegial relationships. Challenging long-held beliefs and confronting less than successful practices require a degree of courage. The mindsets of intense moral purpose, trust and inquiry are all required when challenging theories of action. When disagreements about theories of action are framed as theory competitions rather than as personality differences, trusting relationships can be maintained and critical thinking can take place. Prior agreement about the use of the four standards of accuracy, effectiveness, coherence and improvability can provide school leadership teams with the tools needed to determine the strengths and weaknesses of competing strategies or approaches.

In healthy inquiring learning communities, disagreements about practices, problem seeking and problem solving can truly be a way of life – if trust is intact and if the disagreements focus on theory differences rather than on individuals. Once theory competition is conceptualized as a challenge of ideas, it is less personalized. The evaluation standards provide a way of resolving disagreements by providing external reference points for the discussions of practice.

Developing skill and confidence in problem–based inquiry takes practice. Leaders might consider identifying an issue that is less personal to individual teacher practice but still of reasonable importance as a place to start. One new leader was curious about why lunch hour was structured in such a way that the children raced through their lunches, threw most of them in the garbage and then were hungry and agitated in the afternoon. Another leader wondered about why the lockers in a secondary school were assigned in a particular fashion that kept groups segregated by age. Did this build a sense of community? A third raised the issue of how teachers new to the building were often assigned the least desirable teaching spaces. Applying the standards of accuracy, effectiveness, coherence and improvability in these situations can provide a base for addressing more substantive issues related to student learning.

Leaders with an inquiry mindset know that one of their key tasks is to create a trusting, respectful culture where critically examining practice in pursuit of improving student outcomes becomes the norm. With time, commitment, practice and adherence to standards for critical inquiry, this can become a reality. In addition to the use of narrative, appreciative and problem-based inquiry, leaders also need to harness the power of reflective inquiry to deepen and extend their own thinking.

Reflective inquiry

Cathy was enjoying a few minutes to herself as she walked down the hall on the way to a primary classroom. She was thinking about some agenda items for the final staff meeting on Friday, the family appreciation evening on Tuesday, the school assembly on Wednesday and the Year 7 leaving ceremony on Thursday. She knew these events were important and would provide her with an opportunity to reinforce the values of social responsibility and positive citizenship that the school staff had been working hard to develop. She reminded herself that she also needed to get to the court hearing on Thursday to testify to the events surrounding a fire at the school earlier in the year. She wondered how she would be able to get it all done.

She brought her thoughts back to her remarks for the ceremony for the Year 7s who were leaving for secondary school. She was hopeful that the shared efforts to improve their reading comprehension strategies, their focus on self and peer assessment and their work on developing a greater sense of personal and community responsibility would help them make the transition. As she thought about what she would say, she felt both pleased with the progress the school staff was making and impatient for stronger learning results for her students; however, she knew that after two years of hard work, the school was becoming healthier and more productive. She was looking forward to meeting Debbie for coffee after school on Friday to talk about her next steps.

Suddenly Cathy's thoughts were interrupted by an urgent message – a child had fallen down and was unconscious on the playground. She was needed immediately.

Schools are full of ill-structured and complex problems. The challenges are dynamic in nature. The school leader is often faced with events that demand their immediate attention – from students, staff, parents and other people in the local authority or district organization. Rarely do plans unfold entirely the way they were visualized and school leaders learn to adapt their plans while in motion around unfolding issues. They have to stop (albeit briefly) and think about their actions as they are performing them. This reality is captured in Schön's (1983) useful concept of 'reflection in action'. The reflective practitioner as described by Schön (1987) is a leader who builds a repertoire through inquiry and who uses the practice of reflection to gain insight into leadership actions and events.

We know that successful problem-solvers take time to plan and reflect on their actions. The reality of schools is such that leaders are often dealing with multiple problems simultaneously. They are required to plan and reflect at the same time as they are making decisions. We have seen that one of the powerful distinctions between successful and less successful school leaders is not related to their ability to solve problems but how they reformulate – or think about – problems. Instead of seeing every problem as unique, leaders can start to see problems as examples of a larger type and can draw on past experience to help them make sense of the current issue. Reflective inquiry can help leaders develop the ability to reformulate problems productively.

Studies of how experts engage in sense-making in several different fields underscore the importance of developing meta-cognitive awareness of what takes place during problem solving (Zimmerman 1986; Hutchins 1995; Bransford, Brown and Cocking 1999). Reflective inquiry encompasses both effective inquiry strategies including systematically collecting and interpreting data; and reflective activities, such as monitoring, periodically evaluating progress and revising plans. Reflective inquiry draws attention to connecting meta-cognition and curiosity in the context of solving open-ended, ill structured problems.

Reflection can take different forms. Some leaders find that getting to school extra early gives them a chance to think through the issues facing them. Others use a journal and spend some time on the weekend writing to make meaning. Some meditate or run regularly. Whatever form it takes, reflection should not be seen as a luxury in the midst of an action-filled life, but as a necessity. In addition to private and individual approaches to reflection, we have found that those school leaders who work with an external colleague who will both ask probing questions and listen intently, are better equipped to reframe and then solve important problems of leadership practice.

Helping leaders to be reflective in their work through engaging them in meta-cognitive activities is one of the key features of Jan Robertson's (2008) approach to coaching leadership. Reflection is especially important at pivotal places in school life such as when leaders are trying to modify unsuccessful strategies.

> Reflecting on experiences and action related to them helps leaders become more receptive to trying out new strategies and behaviors. It can also see them changing a value or a belief and, in turn, future actions. Sometimes, however, leaders do not find it easy to reflect adequately on a particular experience and this is where coaches are so useful. Through careful questioning and prompting – direct challenge even, where warranted – they can help leaders more readily relive an experience or look at it differently.
>
> (p. 33)

Based on our own leadership experiences and studies, we believe that leaders who are aware of what Hutchins (1995) describes as the complex dynamics of cognition-in-the-wild are better equipped to bring thinking and acting together in their leadership work. At the very least, they will be less surprised when faced with complex and dynamic issues. Reflective inquiry can also contribute to developing the kind of adaptive expertise required to deal simultaneously with the complexity of human relationships and system improvement.

A spiral of inquiry

The best leaders know how to use a variety of forms of inquiry and can draw on the traditions of narrative, appreciative, problem-based and reflective inquiry to consider and then shift the developmental level of their staff in their unique school contexts. Scholars and theorists can appropriately dedicate themselves to exploring the strengths of a single approach; outstanding practitioner leaders weave the strengths of the approaches most suitable to their cultures together, in order to create new and deeper forms of improvement for young and adult learners. Leaders use the elements of the inquiry mindset as an art form.

We suggest in the title of this chapter that an inquiry mindset implies questions before and during direction setting. Reacting to the external push for accountability, some districts have developed elaborate planning models, provided 'training' for principals in 'smart' goal-setting and demanded 'data-driven' decision-making. We do not disagree with either the value of goal-setting processes or the careful consideration of important and relevant student learning and community satisfaction evidence. Our experience leads us to concur, however, with those who state somewhat wryly that the length and complexity of a school growth plan is generally in inverse proportion to its impact on learning. We have observed many schools where the volume of data has overwhelmed and paralysed the thinking of the staff and hence made genuine improvement less likely. We believe that leaders who begin with questions and actively use multiple forms of inquiry are able to make the direction-setting process more meaningful, more inclusive and ultimately more productive for the learners they serve. An inquiry-oriented approach to improving learning is not linear, sequential, or fully predictable.

Conceptualizing inquiry as a cycle and a spiral has been helpful to many of the leaders with whom we work. The key aspects of a spiral of inquiry focused on improving student learning are reflected in Figure 4.2. In Chapter 7, Learning-Oriented Design, we will build on this spiral of inquiry and will look at the connection between identified learner needs and teacher professional learning.

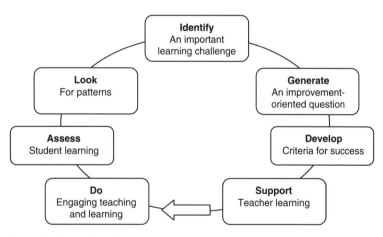

Figure 4.2 Spiral of inquiry.

Conclusion

To make the substantive changes required to move a school from a focus on sorting to a powerful emphasis on learning, leaders require a mindset of intense moral purpose. Building commitment to change and improvement requires positive relationships and for this, the mindset of trust is essential. A leader with an inquiry mindset approaches school transformation through curiosity and a desire for greater knowledge. Leaders listen to the narratives and ask themselves how they can develop a new storyline; they bring an appreciative perspective to their work in creating a clear picture of the ideal they are striving for; they don't back away from applying a critical lens to challenge theories of action; and finally, they find opportunities for reflection both individually and with trusted colleagues.

Leading a school focused on learning requires leaders to know a great deal about learning. Although this may seem somewhat self-evident, it is our experience that while many educators know a great deal about teaching, many know less about learning. Regardless of the reason, we believe that creating genuine learning systems requires school leaders with knowledge about both effective teaching and current approaches to learning. So, in Chapter 5 we will build on the previous mindsets of intense purpose, trust and inquiry by exploring current theories and frameworks for learning that will help you provide the kind of intellectual stimulation your teachers – and your learners – deserve.

Questions for consideration

1   What is the dominant narrative right now in your school? Is it one of enthusiasm, optimism and energy? Is it one of apathy, cynicism or discouragement? Who are the heroes and villains of the school stories? What are you doing to shape the dominant narrative through the stories you tell? What is the story you would like to create?

2   How could you use the dimensions of appreciative inquiry to unleash additional potential in your school?

3   Inquiry is also about asking the 'hard' questions. What connections do you see between the mindsets of moral purpose, trust and inquiry? How could you use the problem-based standards to encourage open, honest dialogue?

4   What forms of reflective inquiry work best for you? Is it through a personal journal? Thinking quietly as you go for a long walk? Conversation with a trusted fried? Meeting with a reflective coaching partner? How can you use reflective inquiry to enhance and deepen your own inquiry mindset?

Chapter 5

Learning for deeper understanding

There is a sense in which teachers' thinking and regulating activity in the classroom needs to operate on at least two levels at the same time: moving between the learning itself and learning how to learn.

Mary James (2007, p. 218)
Improving Learning How to Learn

One of the things a person learns in the process of learning in depth is how claims to knowing can be built and attacked and defended – it's all part of the slow process of discovering the insecurity of our claims to know. Knowing something in depth is like knowing it from the inside, where the student comes to gain expertise and comes to recognize from one area studied in depth something about how knowledge works in all areas.

Kieran Egan (forthcoming, 2009, p. 7)
Learning in Depth: A simple proposal that could transform the experience of schooling

Geoff is a new secondary principal with a strong teaching background in literacy and performing arts. He has seen from his own teaching practice the positive impact that learner engagement makes on motivation and persistence. He enjoys using metaphor and story to hook the imaginations of his students. In his teaching, Geoff creates challenges that demand learner resourcefulness and personal resilience. He believes that effort, not aptitude is the determining factor in learner success and he wants learners increasingly to set their own goals, monitor them and take control of their own learning. He knows that formative assessment practices have a powerful impact on student learning and motivation and he is curious about the extent to which formative assessment is a way of life in his new school.

Geoff visits classrooms regularly and talks with young people about their learning. He observes classrooms where learners are deeply engaged and he also sees classrooms where learners are simply going through the motions, or even worse, have given up. He wonders what he can do to develop greater enthusiasm for learning and deeper learning – in every classroom – for every student. From his recent graduate work, Geoff knows that he is supposed to be a learning leader and actively involved in the professional learning programme. He is starting to wonder whether he actually knows enough about learning to fulfill this critical aspect of his new role effectively. Fortunately for Geoff, his trusted learning partner Anne is also interested in becoming more informed about contemporary learning theories, principles and frameworks. They are both determined to engage in more productive learning-focused conversations with their colleagues and students. Geoff is also realistic – he knows that his new school has a culture where substantive discussions of learning between teachers and between teachers and formal leaders have been infrequent at best.

We believe that school leaders need to be knowledgeable about contemporary approaches to learning if they are to make the shift from a focus on sorting to a passionate commitment to learning. Leaders must be able to extend and deepen teachers' explicit knowledge of learning through professional dialogue. They also need to know the current research on assessment *for* and *as* learning and understand the connections among assessment practices, motivation and engagement. Learning-focused leaders model life-long learning in their own quest for current and emerging sources of knowledge and deeper levels of understanding. As Daniel Schwartz (2005) and his colleagues suggest in their work on the connections between efficiency and innovation, school leaders have to learn to leave the comfortable area of efficiency and move towards a zone of innovation, which may make them feel like uncomfortable novices (2005, p. 30). Geoff will have to learn some new concepts, form some new habits and create new forms of ongoing dialogue if he is to influence his staff in becoming more learning-focused.

Researchers on school leadership are increasingly paying attention to the connection between leadership and learning. In a major study of urban school improvement in the United States, the research team of Penny Sebring, Elaine Allensworth, Anthony Bryk, John Easton and

Stuart Luppescu (2006) concluded that strong learning-focused school leadership is one of five essential supports for improving learning:

> In their leadership role, principals must play a significant role in focusing teachers' and parents' energies on the quality of instruction and the ultimate prize, student learning. To accomplish this aspect of their role principals must be knowledgeable about how children learn, capable of leading discussion and analysis of the curriculum and responsive to teachers' needs for appropriate materials and professional development. They must set high standards for teaching and encourage teachers to take risks and try new methods. Regular visits to classrooms demonstrate their conviction and give them a pulse on daily instruction.
>
> (2006, p. 10)

In a recent book *Powerful Learning: What We Know About Teaching for Understanding*, Linda Darling Hammond (2008) and her colleagues focus primarily on classroom practices that support more powerful learning for students and they acknowledge that to do so requires that schools that have a coherent focus from one classroom to another. 'Schools that redesign their work around student learning spend a great deal of time thinking through what they value, how they will know if they've achieved it and what they must do to create connected learning experiences that enable students to achieve these goals.' (2008, p. 206). In our case study schools, we have found that teachers express respect for principals who are redesigning their work around student learning. These principals are current in their understandings about learning theory and research, can talk informally about learning and demonstrate their enthusiasm for learning through regular informal visits to classrooms. Teachers appreciate the kind of intellectual companionship these principals provide. By being knowledgeable about learning theory and applying learning principles in their own practice, leaders demonstrate their commitment to developing the professional learning programme. They are also demonstrating competence in a core area of their leadership responsibilities. This increases their trustworthiness as described in Chapter 3. Knowledgeable leaders know what matters in teaching and learning (they can 'walk the talk') and as a result they are more able to deepen and extend teacher learning.

In Chapter 1 we emphasized the necessity for schools to make the shift from a focus on sorting students to deep learning for all. We then suggested that intense moral purpose and passionate commit-ment to creating learning for all learners are 'basic' requirements for school leaders. In this chapter we argue that unless principals are well grounded in contemporary knowledge about learning, it is unlikely that the shift from sorting to learning will take place. An emphasis on deep learning has implications for the role of young people in schools. Their role shifts from that of student to one of a learner. Table 5.1 illustrates these shifts.

In considering these shifts, leaders need to understand that learner autonomy and teamwork are not contradictory concepts. As Mary James (2007) points out:

> The ultimate goal of learning how to learn is to promote learning autonomy. This is not quite the same as 'independent learning' or learning in isolation from others. This is hardly ever the case and the concept of 'autonomous learning' should be seen as applying to groups as well as individuals. The important point is that learners take responsibility for their learning (demonstrate agency) and develop strategies that enable them to learn both on their own and interdependently.
>
> (p. 214)

Table 5.1 Shifting from sorting to learning – implications for learners

From Students	To Learners
Dependency	Greater autonomy *and* teamwork
Learning presented as 'work' and 'tasks'	Deep learning outcomes worth doing Goals and learning intentions explicit
Covering	Inquiring
Avoiding challenge	Accepting challenge
Extrinsic motivation and rewards for 'performing'	Intrinsic motivation and recognition of learning growth
Texts, print materials and traditional learning resources provided by teachers	Learners accessing a range of resources and developing sophistication in determining valid sources of information and wisdom

This chapter will provide short summaries of three perspectives on learning theory and key contemporary learning principles that school leaders with whom we work have found particularly useful. In addition, you will have the opportunity to examine four models for learning. Each of these frameworks has implications for changed assessment practices, which we will be considering in greater depth in the next chapter on the evidence mindset. Here we will simply point out that each of these models places a strong emphasis on learners owning and assessing their learning in a much more self-directed way. We will also follow Geoff's work as he develops his own knowledge of current understandings about learning and puts this into practice in his school.

At a 'motivational' session held at a district professional day during the end of the previous year, the staff had been asked by the facilitator to describe their personal metaphors for teaching and learning. Geoff had attended the session and viewed elaborate drawings of flowers with the buds straining towards the sun of learning, being watered by a caring teacher. He had seen sails filled with wind tacking actively across choppy seas of learning. He had seen images of chaotic swirls of energy gathering and losing momentum. He was trying to keep an open mind and wondered how he could learn more and in greater depth about what was really happening for learners in classrooms. What did these teachers really believe about the nature of learning? Was there a match between their visual images and their actions in their classrooms? Geoff was concerned about the impact of several recent policy announcements urging schools to improve their test scores. What impact were these expectations having on the way teachers approached teaching and learning?

Perspectives on learning

Teaching is based on assumptions about how people learn but frequently these assumptions are not explicit nor are they based on sound evidence. One view is that children's minds are metaphorically like somewhat empty vessels that need to be 'filled' with facts presented by teachers. Unfortunately, there are still a number of educators and parents who hang on to this folkloric perspective, which is mainly about teaching and memorizing and has little to do with learning. Three main perspectives on learning have been identified by writers on learning theory (Bransford, Brown and Cocking 1999; Watkins 2003; Watkins, Carnell and Lodge 2007).

Behaviourism, the first of these perspectives, is more concerned with changing behaviour than with deepening thinking. There are several implications for teaching and assessment from a behaviourist perspective: rewards are potent means to establish desired behaviours; breaking learning up into parts and teaching and testing the parts separately is the best way to teach a complex skill; and learning facts and basic skills precedes understanding. Although this theory has fallen out of favor as the dominant theory for education, many practices associated with it are still widespread in schools. Our experience is that under system stress or personal pressure, teachers, leaders and systems often fall back on a more behaviourist approach and the policies and assessment practices that are associated with it. Overly intense external accountability policies seem to increase the use of behaviourist styles in schools.

A second perspective, constructivism, looks at learning through a focus on the thinking process and how learners operate cognitively. Constructivists are concerned with the mental models that learners use when responding to new information or new problems. Fundamental to constructivism is the belief that learning always involves analysing and transforming new information. Transforming new ideas can only be achieved based on what the learner already knows and understands. This implies that teaching must begin by exploring prior knowledge and understanding. Constructivists argue that, unless learners make their thinking explicit to others and to themselves, they cannot become aware of the need to modify their ideas or concepts. This implies that students need to understand what it means to learn and they need to monitor how they go about planning and revising, to reflect upon their learning and to learn to determine for themselves whether or not they understand. This demands both self-awareness and self-regulation.

A third, social constructivist perspective, extends these ideas primarily based on the thinking of the Russian psychologist, Lev Vygotsky (1978), who emphasized that an important characteristic of learning is that it develops in a social context through interaction between the teacher or a more expert peer and the learner. Learning is mediated by language and promoted by social norms that value the search for understanding. As we look later in this chapter and the next at the impact of assessment on motivation and engagement, it is important to note that most approaches to assessment for learning have been developed within a cognitive constructivist framework. More recently, however, Paul Black and Dylan Wiliam (2006) have begun to develop a theory of formative assessment drawing more on socio-cultural perspectives (James et al, 2007, p. 18).

Recent developments in learning theory reflect the observation that people learn through participating in communities of practice, somewhat like apprentices. Through membership and activity they come to understand what to pay attention to and what counts as quality in a particular group. This is an important consideration for teachers since what might be valued in one subject may not be the same in another. Writing descriptive prose in a literature class is generally quite different than writing a lab report in a science course or designing a web page or a dance sequence. The role of the leader as intellectual companion to teachers is enhanced when he or she understands and can identify and discuss the learning theory that underlies an individual teacher's approach. This under-standing can provide a productive starting point for extending teacher thinking. In addition to understanding theories of learning, a solid understanding of the learning principles derived from con-temporary studies of the learning process will also assist leaders in their work. Using concepts based on the learning principles in discussions, demonstrations and professional learning sessions can help to develop the school learning programme and the professional confidence of the staff.

Learning principles

Geoff spent at least an hour every day visiting classrooms, talking to learners and chatting informally with teachers. Although somewhat cautious at first, teachers gradually welcomed his visits as an opportunity to share what their learners were doing and where they were going next with their learning. Anne and Geoff knew it was important to limit judging words in these conversations with either teachers or learners. Instead of hearing themselves use words like 'Great job' or 'Excellent' they agreed to describe in their own words the principles of learning that they saw were evident – and let the teachers draw their own conclusions. 'Maria, I see that you have used at least two strategies successfully in figuring out that problem. Can you tell me how you decided that these ones would work for you?' 'Mr Sola, Sandra seems very engaged with her group and seems to be making a positive contribution. I know she has struggled with Physics before. What made the difference for her?' 'Ranjeev, your parents told me how much they appreciated the work you did on helping them apply for their passports. How challenging was it for you to work in Punjabi on this project?'

In recent years, the broader teaching and learning research communities have been paying considerably more attention to new understandings from psychology, sociology and brain research. At the same time, researchers, concerned about educational reform policies in a number of countries, are mobilizing their efforts to encourage a more informed policy environment. A group of American researchers with a strong background in learning theory worked for many years to develop a living document about what is currently known about learning, motivation, personal and social development and individual differences. Barbara McCombs (2003) and her colleagues have distilled this knowledge into a set of principles designed to inform curriculum development work and classroom instruction. These principles, summarized in Table 5.2, can also supply a useful starting point for leaders in day-to-day conversations with teachers and with learners. They provide a helpful lens for school leaders who are exploring various learning frameworks and thinking about the assessment practices used in their schools. You will find that these principles are emphasized to varying degrees in each of the models presented later in this chapter.

Many school leaders we have observed have taken the core ideas underlying the principles and personalized them in language that is accessible for teachers and learners. In these schools, teachers report that their principals are better equipped to lead thoughtful learning conversations and to guide intelligent practice. In our experience, leaders with a solid working knowledge of contemporary learning theory and learning principles are also better equipped to have more persuasive dialogues with senior leaders and policymakers about accountability policies and testing practices.

In the next section, we will outline four models or frameworks for thinking about learning that school leaders are finding useful in designing their professional learning programmes. Although each of these models uses a somewhat different vocabulary, many of the concepts are complementary and are connected to the principles of learning. As you consider each of these models, think about the connections with the learning principles and reflect on your own school context. Which of these models do you think would be most relevant to the learners you serve? Consider the knowledge base of the teachers with whom you work and how you might help them become more explicit in their understanding of current learning concepts. Our summaries of these learning models are by necessity very brief and we encourage you to consider

Table 5.2 Learning principles

COGNITIVE AND META-COGNITIVE FACTORS

Principle 1: Nature of the learning process The learning of complex subject matter is most effective when it is an intentional process of constructing meaning from information and experience.

Principle 2: Goals of the learning process The successful learner, over time and with support and instructional guidance, can create meaningful, coherent representations of knowledge.

Principle 3: Construction of knowledge The successful learner can link new information with existing knowledge in meaningful ways.

Principle 4: Strategic thinking The successful learner can create and use a repertoire of thinking and reasoning strategies to achieve complex learning goals.

Principle 5: Thinking about thinking Higher-order strategies for selecting and monitoring mental operations facilitate creative and critical thinking.

Principle 6: Context of learning Learning is influenced by environmental factors, including culture, technology, and instructional practices.

MOTIVATION AND AFFECTIVE FACTORS

Principle 7: Motivational and emotional influences on learning
What, and how much is learned, is influenced by the learner's motivation. Motivation to learn, in turn, is influenced by the individual's emotional states, beliefs, interests, goals and habits of thinking.

Principle 8: Intrinsic motivation to learn The learner's creativity, higher order thinking, and natural curiosity all contribute to motivation to learn. Intrinsic motivation is stimulated by tasks of optimal novelty and difficulty, relevant to personal interests, and providing for personal choice and control.

Principle 9: Effects of motivation on effort Acquisition of complex knowledge and skills requires extended learner effort and guided practice. Without learner's motivation to learn, the willingness to exert this effort is unlikely without coercion.

(Continued Overleaf)

Table 5.2 Continued

DEVELOPMENTAL AND SOCIAL FACTORS

Principle 10: Developmental influence on learning As individuals develop, they encounter different opportunities and experience different constraints for learning. Learning is most effective when differential development within and across physical, intellectual, emotional and social domains is taken into account.

Principle 11: Social influences on learning Learning is influenced by social interactions, interpersonal relations and communication with others.

INDIVIDUAL DIFFERENCES FACTORS

Principle 12: Individual differences in learning Learners have different strategies, approaches, and capabilities for learning that are a function of prior experience and heredity.

Principle 13: Learning and diversity Learning is most effective when differences in learners' linguistic, cultural and social backgrounds are taken into account.

Principle 14: Standards and assessment Setting appropriately high and challenging standards and assessing the learner and learning progress – including diagnostic, process and outcome assessments – are integral parts of the learning process.

Table adapted from McCombs, B.L. (2003) A framework for the redesign of K-12 education in the context of current educational reform. *Theory into Practice*, (42) 2, pp. 329–337.

these descriptions simply as a starting point in deepening your knowledge.

Learning models

When Geoff reviewed report cards he was struck by the inconsistency in the learning results for a number of students. Anne encouraged him to look more closely at the connection between motivation and classroom assessment practices. He thought about Miguel, a 15-year-old who had just competed in a technology Olympiad with his solar-powered car. Miguel had spent countless hours after school working on his designs and getting coaching from

Mr Herbert. Why couldn't this enthusiasm and hard work carry over into History, where he was behind on assignments and in danger of failing? During rehearsals for the school musical 'Little Shop of Horrors', Geoff got to know Aimee, a 14-year-old with real drive. He watched her carefully work through every scene. He saw how closely she listened and followed directions. He wondered whether this was the same girl that Mme Dubois complained about for her inattention to detail in her Art class. And he thought about Sam, a young boy with an obvious passion and talent in Science. He saw the way Sam had meticulously prepared for his presentation on penguins and he wondered why this passion did not carry over to English or into the gym.

Effort-based learning

International comparisons of school improvement have raised questions about the ways in which learners in different cultures attribute success – and the role of effort. In many western, English-speaking countries, success is deemed to be mainly a result of aptitude. By contrast, in many Asian nations, success is attributed to the degree of effort made by the learner and teacher working together. Lauren Resnick (1995), an American psychologist and researcher, has invested many years of work in developing a learning model with a clear focus on effort. She has subsequently worked with many schools and districts in the United States to implement the nine main learning beliefs in her model. To do justice to all of the concepts is beyond the scope of this chapter. What follows are four of the concepts that leaders we work with have found particularly useful in shifting practices in their school towards a stronger learning orientation.

An important concept in this model is that learner effort is at the centre of success in learning in any area. An effort-based school emphasizes the importance of sustained and directed effort resulting in a deeper level of understanding for all learners, as opposed to a belief that individual aptitude determines what and how much students learn. Leaders implementing this model make sure that everything about the school programme is organized to support the belief that effort is expected and that tough learning problems are solved through sustained work. Every learner is taught an intellectually challenging curriculum that is matched to high standards and is provided with as much time and expert teaching as he or she needs to meet or exceed expectations.

A second key concept is that learners need clear expectations along with fair and credible assessment practices. Because all learners are expected to learn concepts at a high level of challenge, clear expectations of what is to be learned are provided for faculty, parents, community members and, most important, for the learners themselves. Descriptive criteria and models of learner work that meet the criteria are displayed publicly and used by learners to help them analyse and discuss their work. Learners are assisted in evaluating their own work and in setting individual goals for their next steps through their ability to access clearly visible examples of good work. Evaluations are fair because projects, classroom assessments, performances and tests are all connected to the curriculum and to clear standards for success. Grading practices are referenced to clear standards rather than on a curve, so learners can readily see the connection between their own effort and their results. Learners know how they are being evaluated and they know how to prepare for evaluation tasks.

A third important idea in the effort-based learning model is that thinking and problem solving constitute the 'new basics' for the 21st century. Thinking requires a solid foundation of knowledge. Engaging learners in thinking involves teaching a curriculum organized around major concepts that students are expected to learn deeply – one that engages students in active reasoning about these concepts. In every subject, at every grade level, learning and teaching demands an active application of knowledge through challenging thinking. Curriculum practices are shifted so that fewer concepts are considered and deeper exploration of the concepts is made possible.

A fourth major idea is that learning requires talk with others. From the effort-based perspective, however, not all talk sustains learning. For classroom dialogue to promote learning it must be accountable. Accountable conversation responds seriously to what others in the group have said and further develops the ideas put forth. It demands contributions that are accurate and relevant to the issue under discussion. Accountable talk uses evidence appropriate to the discipline such as proof in math, inquiry data in science, text details in literature and documents in history and follows established norms of good reasoning. Teachers intentionally foster the norms of evidence appropriate to each area and learners develop the skills of thoughtful, discipline-related dialogue in their classrooms.

Self-regulated learning

The self-regulated learning model is concerned with the contexts, environments and social and cognitive factors that guide and encourage learning. In this model teachers and principals pay attention to the learning conditions that promote successful learning and are alert to those conditions that make academic self-regulation difficult. School leaders interested in making self-regulated learning central to their school's culture, focus on the development of learner self-directedness in approaching new learning. This includes developing an individual profile of the motivation and strategic repertoire of each learner in a key area, such as reading for information. These profiles then form the focus for professional learning work and dialogue about teaching approaches that increase learner independence.

Educators focus directly on learner self-regulation by concerning themselves with the processes used by learners in setting goals, monitoring and controlling their own learning, paying attention to their own motivations and actions in learning and generally observing how learners guide their own actions, in the pursuit of deeper levels of understanding. For example, school leaders in British Columbia and Quebec have drawn on the work of two Canadian researchers, Deborah Butler and Sylvie Cartier (2005), who have developed secondary reading profiles for students both in schools where learners were struggling and in schools where learners found academic work relatively easy.

As part of this work, Butler and Cartier (2005) developed a six-part model of self-regulated learning and several user-friendly surveys that leaders and teachers can utilize as a part of their exploration of their learners' approaches to intellectual work. Among the six aspects they suggest educators consider is context, which they define as the multiple layers that form the framework for student learning. They note that the context of the district, the neighborhood of the school, the nature of the classroom and the area of learning all have an influence on learner self-regulation.

They also stress the importance of paying attention to individual learners and their unique histories of learning strengths, difficulties, preferences and interests that together shape how they approach learning in new areas. What individual learners themselves bring to each learning context is important. Butler and Cartier (2005) note that there are important mediating factors that affect learner self-regulation. Learners are influenced by their perceptions of the difficulty or complexity of tasks, by their beliefs about their own competence and control and by their conceptions of what is involved in the learning, as well as by their degree of background knowledge. In addition, the nature of their emotional reactions to learning is important; the emotional state of the learner before, during and after engaging in a learning sequence all have an impact. The manner in which assessment and classroom interaction patterns are handled also have a major influence on the perceptions of possible success by learners.

Two additional important variables in this model are how learners interpret tasks and how they set their own personal objectives. As an important self-regulation process, learners draw on their experiences to interpret the demands involved in a particular task. This interpretation influences how learners set goals, choose strategies and use criteria to self-assess their progress in achieving the desired learning outcome. Consciously or unconsciously, learners then set objectives to achieve what they understand the task expectations to be. In many cases, when learners are discouraged by the task, they direct their attention to protecting their emotional well-being by avoiding a focus on intellectual outcomes. In other cases, when learners are positive about both the learning expectations and the task at hand, they make plans for their use of the resources of time and materials, select strategies for task completion, self-monitor their progress, adjust their plans and self-evaluate using criteria and any feedback they receive.

The final aspect of the self-regulated model is the use by the learner of cognitive strategies. How learners select and use cognitive strategies to accomplish tasks is important. Once learners have determined what they believe the task to be, they identify strategies they think will help them to meet the requirements. For the greatest success in learning, a learner needs to select a strategy that matches the task demand involved. Whether they are reading a lab report or reading a poem, they must bring their own strengths to the work, find multiple ways to complete the task and then use one that is the best fit such as using an outline or a graphic organizer.

The six aspects of this model demonstrate the complexity of the learning required. As Butler and Cartier (2005) point out:

> The most academically successful learners are often more consciously aware of managing their learning activities and take control of self-directing their efforts. For example, these learners may take the time to deliberately interpret tasks and

make plans, think about strategy alternatives, interpret feedback they are given to derive directions for further learning, or self-monitor and manage emotions.

(p. 4)

Many less successful learners in schools lack conscious knowledge of how and when to self-regulate their learning to accomplish the learning tasks at hand. For learners without this knowledge, the self-regulated model offers a productive starting point in providing information that they can use to take a more positive and active role in their learning. For teachers, self-regulation involves engaging in continuous reflection on learning and teaching practices, and on identifying underlying assumptions. Teachers are expected to identify thoughtful teaching and learning practices, plan using these practices, apply their thinking in the classroom and monitor and critically reflect on the learning outcomes. In this model there is a very strong emphasis on involving learners in strategy building and goal selection and on the importance of embedding strategic discussions in meaningful learning work. Learner independence is a critically important feature of self-regulated learning.

The links in practice between the design of adult professional learning and learner self-regulation have also been explored:

> Emerging professional development models have the potential, not just to promote teachers' use of effective instructional approaches, but to support them to reflect on and revise teaching practices so as to construct new conceptual knowledge. There are also multiple benefits to working collectively to define and revise one's practices. Through social interaction, benefits may be accrued in the richness of conceptual understandings co-constructed with others and sustained commitment to innovation.
>
> (Butler et al. 2004, p. 440)

Self-regulated learning is concerned with the development of independent, confident learners by providing teachers with a set of lenses to understand the conditions that promote successful learning. Effort-based learning is focused on shifting learners' and teachers' attribution of success from aptitude to effort. Imaginative learning sets forth the challenge to teachers of engaging learners through imagination and creativity. Let's look next at what this model has to offer.

Geoff was learning a great deal from his discussions with Anne, from the readings they were sharing and from his conversations with teachers and learners. He was pleased that members of the Social Studies and Mathematics departments were building time into their weekly meetings to consider ideas about effort-based learning and self-regulation. He was encouraged when the English department chair asked him if he could provide copies of a book on formative assessment in secondary schools for each of the teachers.

Geoff was also thinking carefully about the many imaginative strategies he saw in place in classrooms and was wondering how he might be able to generate momentum about engaging more learners in such imaginative ways. He smiled when he thought of the Science class where learners were designing robots to do household chores. He hoped they would have a design ready soon! He was only slightly chagrined when he remembered how he got so caught up in the students' stories of the children of migrant workers in Ms Craig's class that he forgot to attend a budget meeting. He had been completely drawn into the debate that he saw in a Geography class when learners were arguing climate change through the lenses of security and fear. How could he build on these engaging practices? Anne told him that she had just recently discovered some very helpful resources on the web about imaginative learning and suggested that Geoff should take a look.

Imaginative learning

The imaginative learning model is based the concepts of a Canadian theoretician, Kieran Egan, who argues in his book *An Imaginative Approach to Teaching* (2005) that educators need to think much less about prior knowledge and much more about how to engage the imaginations of their learners. Egan was curious to discover if teachers could get learners more engaged in their learning if they first considered tapping into their imaginations rather than exploring what learners already knew – or thought they knew. There is growing international interest in Egan's imaginative model and there is a particularly strong interest in this approach in jurisdictions serving indigenous learners, since it fits well with an emphasis on oral storytelling and on a deep appreciation of the natural world. Educators with an interest in the arts are also drawn to this model, as are many teachers and leaders whose interests lie in math, science and history. Educators and researchers exploring this set of ideas have formed an international study group, the Imaginative Education Research Group (IERG) and are considering ideas about learning from the following perspective:

Imagination is the ability to think of what might be possible, in a manner that is not tightly constrained by the actual or taken-for-granted. It is the 'reaching out' feature of the mind, enabling us to go beyond what we have mastered so far. Without human imagination, no culture would look the way it does today and no learner would be able to participate in and contribute to that culture.

(www.ierg.org accessed 14 July 2008)

Practitioners who work from an imaginative perspective argue that one of the strengths of the imaginative model is that, unlike the current behaviourist or memorization-based models seen in many schools and systems, it corresponds more closely to how learners acquire more lasting understandings of the world. They hypothesize that educators need a model that helps learners apply their thinking to new situations and challenges by generating understandings that are both flexible and lasting. Educators who work with an imaginative learning model place a strong emphasis on two key areas. The first is on the power of oral language and the cognitive early language tools that are especially important before literacy skills become fluent. The second is on the cognitive tools that have developed over human cultural history as aids to the thinking and understanding of learners. The cognitive tools in the imaginative repertoire are used across the curriculum and at all stages of the learning process. Some of these key tools include stories, the use of binary opposites and images.

Imaginative educators view stories as one of the strongest cognitive tools for engaging learners of all ages with knowledge. Stories play a key role in shaping the emotional understanding of factual and fictional material and have educational power because they are able to simultaneously engage the emotions and the imaginations of the learner as important curriculum concepts are explored in depth. A second important cognitive tool is the use of abstract binary opposites, which are used in organizing and categorizing knowledge. Imaginative theorists suggest that opposites are in conflict in most fictional stories and are crucial in providing an initial ordering to many complex forms of knowledge. 'The most powerfully engaging opposites – like good/bad, security/fear, competition/cooperation – are emotionally charged and, when attached to curriculum content, imaginatively engaging.' (Egan 2005, p. 3).

Imaginative educators contend that the ability of the learner to make differentiations in the form of contradictories (this is A; this is not A) is fundamental to all cognitive processes. A third important tool is the generation of mental images from words. Imaginative educators argue that, in a world saturated with media-based images, it is increasingly vital to let learners generate their own unique images since learner-created images have more memorable force and make learning more imaginative and engaging. Teachers using this cognitive tool understand that words can be used to develop images with strong emotional effects in the minds of their learners.

As well as stories, opposites and images, there are additional cognitive tools that imaginative education practitioners are exploring in their learning work including metaphor, movement, rhyme, rhythm and pattern and jokes, gossip and humor. Using all these tools in the imaginative repertoire can help teachers to connect more deeply with the imaginative worlds of young people. Imaginative educators believe it is important for leaders using this model to see the world less from an adult perspective and more from the perspective of learners and what engages them. Actively engaging the full participation of the learner with curriculum content through utilizing the power of imaginative forms of thinking is critical. In Egan's most recent book, *Learning In Depth* (forthcoming, 2009), he extends the thinking in his imaginative model with a provocative yet simple approach to individualizing knowledge building from the earliest stages of formal schooling. The learning in-depth strategy he describes involves the ceremonial assignment of each early learner to a personal topic worthy of pursuit for an extended time period. This is a topic about which the learner will acquire extensive expertise over their whole school experience. Because of Egan's belief that all knowledge is wonderful, he persuasively suggests that learners be provided 'room' to learn and become expert from the start of their formal school experiences.

We believe that leaders with an understanding of the ideas included in effort-based, self-regulated and imaginative learning are much better positioned to provide the kind of intellectual companionship and stimulation that teachers both desire and require. The final model we will describe in this chapter provides a useful framework especially for leaders who are striving to understand exactly what is meant by lifelong learning.

By the end of his first year, Geoff was gaining confidence about his knowledge of learning and his ability to engage teachers in more meaningful conversations about learning. At the same time, he knew that he had only scratched the surface and learning for deep understanding was going to be a long-term venture. He was somewhat amused when Anne provided him with a description of the hare brain and the tortoise mind. He had learned from Anne about the dangers of moving too quickly to judgment and he was well aware of his impatience for quick results. He knew there were going to be many challenges in the years ahead as he shifted his school culture to one of deeper learning. Many school-wide and individual professional conversations were required. Resilience and resourcefulness, reciprocity and reflectiveness were going to be helpful if teachers were to sustain their professional learning and keep the school moving forward.

Lifelong learning

Guy Claxton, author of *Hare Brain, Tortoise Mind: How Intelligence Increases When You Think Less* (1998) and *Building Learning Power* (2002) is deeply interested in issues of creativity and lifelong learning. In his first book he describes the 'hare' brain, with its faster thought-processing speed – a brain that is analytical, calculating and self-conscious. He also describes the 'tortoise' mind, which is slower, more meditative and, in his view, more useful when creative solutions are needed. In his second book he has applied this thinking to lifelong learning for young people in schools.

Claxton (2002) maintains that there are four big learning habits that good lifelong learners need to develop. The first habit is resilience, which involves being ready and willing to focus hard on learning in spite of shifting emotions and multiple distractions. This quality requires absorption, perseverance, attention to patterns and an ability to manage distractions. Learners with resilience like a challenge, like knowing that learning is sometimes hard and are not afraid of making mistakes. Claxton (2002) draws on the work of Carol Dweck in her assertion about resilience:

> It doesn't help a child to tackle a difficult task if they succeed consistently on an easy one. It doesn't teach them to persist in the face of obstacles if the obstacles are always eliminated . . . What children learn best from are slightly difficult tasks which they have to struggle though. Knowing they can cope with difficulties is what makes children seek challenges and overcome further problems.
>
> (p. 20)

The second aspect of a learning-powered mind is resourcefulness. Piaget, the Swiss psychologist, once defined intelligence as knowing what to do when you don't know what to do. According to Claxton (2002), being resourceful means 'having a good repertoire of attitudes and strategies for confronting the world when it becomes strange or out of control' (p. 25). This habit includes questioning and curiosity, making links, imagining, reasoning and capitalizing. He includes rigorous thinking and critiquing as a part of this habit along with the ability to seek out and use a range of people and both traditional and current technological resources.

Reflectiveness is the third habit in Claxton's model, which requires a strategic sense and self-awareness of where you are as a developing learner. He suggests that good learners are intuitive, but they also need to be aware of how their learning is going and make strategic decisions about it (2002, p. 31). Planning, revising, distilling the essential features and meta-learning are a part of this category. Reflective learners are able to change tack when strategies do not seem to be working. According to this model, the skills and dispositions of meta-learning can be cultivated simply by a teacher's use of questions such as 'How did you go about finding that out', or 'How would you go about teaching that to other people?' (2002, p. 35).

The final learning habit is conceptualized as reciprocal relationships, which involves being able to learn from and with others. It includes having the courage of personal convictions and the willingness to collaborate as part of a team. Learners with reciprocity as one of their learning powers are open to the intelligent ways of learning and thinking that others have to share. The components involved in reciprocity include interdependence, collaboration, empathy and listening and imitation.

Discussions about the necessity for lifelong learning abound, but unless there is a way of understanding exactly what is meant by the rhetoric, the term can become an empty one. The leaders with whom we work have found that the four components of lifelong learning – resilience, resourcefulness, reflectiveness and reciprocity – provide a useful and manageable framework for thinking about changes in learning programmes in their schools.

Conclusion

In the learning-oriented mindset, we claim that leaders who are serious about moving their schools from a focus on sorting to a focus on deep learning must first be knowledgeable about learning. One of the chief responsibilities of school leaders is to provide intellectual stimulation to teachers. Simply being present in classrooms, expressing interest in what the teacher is doing, or even worse, engaging in superficial 'walk-throughs' will do little or nothing to deepen and enhance learning. Leaders with a solid understanding of contemporary learning theories and principles, who are able to apply a model that makes sense in the context of the learners, the content area, the classroom and the school will be better able to provide the kind of substantive support teachers and learners deserve.

In addition to knowledge of learning theories, principles and models, leaders need to know what kind of evidence to look for to indicate that learning is actually taking place. We have mentioned in this chapter and elsewhere the importance of formative assessment. Leaders with an evidence-seeking mindset are interested in far more than the data provided by state or provincial assessments. They are determined to find and use the forms of information that will genuinely have an impact on learning and on learners and as a result will build greater confidence in the school and the system. In Chapter 6, we will meet Donna, a secondary vice principal who is determined not to let any learners 'fall through the cracks' and is seeking ways of using evidence to create momentum for action.

Questions for consideration

1   Think about the classrooms or learning areas in your school. In what ways have you seen the learning principles in action? What are you doing to underline for teachers the positive ways in which they are applying these principles? How could you be even more focused in your work to make their tacit knowledge explicit?

2   How is effort acknowledged and encouraged in your school? In what ways do you think your learners would benefit from a greater emphasis on effort-based learning?

3   How is imagination already being used to build learner engagement? How might the learners in your school benefit from a more focused intentionality around imaginative strategies?

4   In what ways do you see teachers encouraging self-regulation among learners? What connections do you see between self-regulation, effort-based and imaginative learning?

5   The term 'lifelong learning' is heard frequently as the underlying concept behind many reform efforts. To what extent are learners building resilience, resourcefulness, reflectiveness and reciprocity as learning powers in your school?

6   Assessment practices such as descriptive feedback have a big effect on learner self-regulation and motivation. Think about the grading and assessment practices in your school. How closely connected are these practices with current understandings about learning? If they are not close, what changes will you consider making?

Chapter 6

Evidence-seeking in action

Educators, whether leaders or teachers, make hundreds of decisions in a day. Not every decision requires a major research study. However, decisions that have far-reaching consequences or are high stakes deserve to be investigated thoroughly through the lenses of pertinent data, as a way of either validating hunches or rethinking ideas.

Lorna Earl and Helen Timperley, (eds) (2008, p 17)
Professional Learning Conversations: Challenges
in Using Evidence for Improvement.

From a sense-making perspective, what is noticed in a school environment, whether this information is understood as evidence pertaining to some problem and how it is eventually used in practice . . . depends on the cognitions of individuals operating within that school . . . Practitioners must notice, frame and interpret new information before they can put it into practice as evidence.

James Spillane and David Miele (2007, p. 46)
Evidence in Practice: A Framing of the Terrain.

Donna Lim was excited. It was the fall of her first year as vice principal at Robert Bell Secondary and she had just returned from a leadership seminar where she had been challenged to think about, and then to act on, the greatest learning challenges in her new school. Her initial impression of the school was one of somewhat self-satisfied complacency. The results were generally good, parents and students were for the most part satisfied and teachers believed that, although not perfect, things were pretty good. She knew from her previous experience as a counsellor in another school and from her initial interactions with learners in the office, in classrooms and in the hallways that there were young people who were struggling and who, without intervention, would either quietly fade out or be subtly – or not so subtly – encouraged to leave school. She spent time chatting with teachers and counsellors and she could see from reading and signing report cards that roughly one quarter of the Year 9 students were on a rocky road. As she thought about these students, she could identify three distinct groups.

A group of girls she privately described as 'fifteen going on thirty' seemed disinterested in anything other than socializing and were well on the road to fading out. A group of boys who were often in minor and sometimes not so minor scraps, she described to herself as 'angry young men'. There was a third group she thought of as 'the lost souls'. For a variety of reasons these young people seemed to be floundering in their learning and in their lives. Now what, she thought? Without some kind of helpful intervention, she was sure these Year 9 learners would drift into school failure. She knew that to generate interest and commitment on the part of her colleagues, it was essential for her to provide convincing evidence about the need for change. Where to begin?

There is a difference between the patterns of evidence that Donna knew would help to mobilize teacher action and the forms of school, district and provincial data that were readily available to her. Access to data was not an issue. The Ministry of Education website was loaded with data. Binders of accumulated school test results weighed down the shelves of her office. Donna's 'data overload' situation is not unique. Despite the urging from researchers and policymakers that leaders become 'data driven', many observers report that they find educators in schools, especially those in jurisdictions with strong external accountability pressures, are sinking under the weight of heavy loads of undigested data. Even where data from a number of levels are made accessible to school leaders, interpreting the evidence and moving to sensible action is a daunting task. School leaders understand that they have a responsibility to use evidence wisely, to consider a variety of data sources and to assist their staffs in using the information to deepen learning and to strengthen social justice. Deciding what to pay attention to, determining meaningful patterns of evidence and learning to facilitate thoughtful, trusting and probing discussions with teachers are challenging and important leadership tasks.

As we have observed schools that are data rich and information poor, we have started to ask two questions: First, what kind of information do school leaders find helpful when looking for evidence of deep learning? And second, how does the leader's perspective about evidence-seeking and evidence use influence the thinking and actions of teachers? In this chapter we are going to look more closely at several aspects of an evidence-informed mindset – a mindset that helps transform evidence into knowledge about patterns and provides directions for meaningful change. First, we will offer a perspective on accountability in a learning system. Then, we will look at how educators are connecting questions about learner engagement with the research and practice evidence on formative assessment and finally, we will look at ways that leaders can help their schools become more evidence-informed.

Accountability for learning

Donna continued to think hard about how to capture the attention of her principal and of her staff. Knowing that the school had been recognized publicly for their completion rates of close to 98 per cent had resulted in some complacency. Having the top student in the last year's provincial Physics exam also was a point of pride for the school. It was only when she dug more deeply into the data that it became clear that the completion rate did not include those learners who disappeared from school before their final year. She also found out that the participation rate in Physics was very low and wondered why there were so few girls enrolled. She phoned some of the young people who had left Robert Bell before graduating. She arranged to meet them in the local coffee shop and she listened intently to their stories. She heard about how they knew school was important and how they all wished they had completed. She heard about the obstacles they faced in their own lives and she learned about those special teachers who had reached out to them. Then she pulled together the three groups of students that she had identified in Year 9. Again, she listened intently as they talked about their experiences in school – what worked to support their learning and what didn't. She wondered what connection there was between the school plan that was supposed to be focusing on increasing academic results and the lived experience of these young people.

School systems worldwide are struggling to develop and implement accountability systems that actually provide useful information both to schools and to the public and create the basis for genuine improvement. We stated in Chapter 1 that part of shifting to a learning system involves a new way of looking at accountability. In the sorting system, common factors include external pressures for accountability in the form of legislation such as No Child Left Behind in the US, formal inspections, external reviews, demands for accountability contracts and extensive school plans submitted to a central authority. Teachers and principals respond in a variety of ways to these external pressures. We have seen responses that range from embracing and developing ownership of the directions to tacit compliance, passive resistance and outright defiance. Sue Lasky, Gene Schaffer and Tim Hopkins (2008), note the following about the US environment:

> A key tension is that the current policy and high stakes accountability context places primacy on systematic reporting of school and district-level data to states and the federal government for accountability purposes. These accountability mandates pressure decision-making, resource use, curriculum changes and staffing but can only be effective at the school level if principals and teachers can clearly see the linkages among policy, curriculum and assessment and how all these add up to improvement. These linkages are not being provided at the national, state and district level to the degree that all schools can understand, or alter, their behaviours to effect change.
>
> (p. 106)

We also agree with Elmore (2003) who has persuasively argued that internal accountability by educators is critically important because 'high internal school agreement is the best defense against uninformed external pressure' (p. 10). In schools led by educators with intense moral purpose and an evidence mindset, there is strong internal ownership for improvement and transformation. In these schools, accountability is not about developing school plans that meet some distant bureaucratic imperative. It is about taking responsibility for genuine learning improvement and building confidence in the identity, direction and learning focus of the school among learners, staff and the community.

Creating a school culture where thoughtful evidence sources are used regularly and seamlessly on a daily, weekly, monthly and annual basis is the goal of the evidence-minded leader. Seeking, organizing and acting on evidence builds levels of coherence and allows the school to focus on important learning agendas even when the specific focus may differ from the dominant policy direction. A strong evidence mindset, high internal agreement and knowledge of learning results serve school leaders well in maintaining their focus and not being derailed by the latest demand. When schools 'own' the information about the learning needs of their young people, they are much more likely to make wise decisions about professional learning programmes and resource materials. They are less likely to be swayed by the current instructional or professional development trend. Leaders in these schools have connected their intense moral purpose and evidence mindset to seek out the most useful information regarding the progress of their learners. They are not obsessed with test scores, nor do they ignore this information. They are most interested in questions such as these:

- How are we doing at increasing both quality and equity?
- How engaged are our learners?
- How can we organize information in useful ways so that it can inform our daily work?
- How can we create the conditions in which it is routine for us as a staff – individually and collectively – to access and use relevant research and practice evidence to inform our teaching?
- How can we make sure that all learners own their learning and are able to articulate what they are learning, how they are learning and what they need to do next to improve?

As leaders start to seriously consider issues of learner engagement, they are drawn to the kind of evidence that can best be gathered directly from learners and from observations in classrooms or other learning settings. More formal data sources such as report cards, results of formal exams or standardized assessment and attitudinal surveys can also provide useful starting places. Understanding the ways that teachers use assessment evidence to inform their instruction can only be understood through dialogue with teachers and learners and through observation in classrooms. The evidence about the impact of formative assessment on learning and motivation (Black and Wiliam 1998, 2006) is compelling. In the learning system, the focus must shift from an overemphasis on assessment *of* learning to a more balanced approach incorporating both assessment *for* learning and assessment *as* learning. In no way can we do justice to the importance of this shift in this book. At best we can either reinforce the direction already underway in many schools or motivate you to look much more closely at the research literature on formative assessment and then the current practice in your school with the goal of having all learners truly understanding how to learn and owning their own learning.

Learner engagement and formative assessment

As Donna moves through the school she can be overheard talking quietly with individual learners. 'Hi Frances, what are you learning in music right now? How is it going?' 'Kate, I enjoyed reading your project on fish farming. Can you tell me what you learned from your research? What do you hope to learn when your class goes to the marine station next week?' 'Hi Gord, I hear that you have been very helpful in coaching Mia on problem-solving. What strategy did you find worked the best?' When Donna finds learners who really understand what they are learning, she makes a point of having a short conversation with the teacher to provide descriptive information about what she has seen and heard. She has noticed that teachers are paying increased attention to clarifying the learning intentions for their classes in the school since she and Dean, her principal, started this practice a few months ago.

Although test data and other quantitative information have an important place in evidence-based conversations, teacher and principal observations are also extremely important. Leaders who focus on learner engagement in their classroom observations demonstrate a desire to know learners and teachers as individuals. Classroom observation focused on learner engagement, done well, can provide a wealth of actionable evidence. Researchers have pointed out the importance of paying attention to whether learners are genuinely engaged. Fredricks (2004) and his colleagues, for example, have noted that 'the concept of school engagement has attracted growing interest as a way to ameliorate low levels of academic achievement, high levels of student boredom and disaffection and high dropout rates in urban areas' (p. 59).

We have mentioned previously the international survey data that indicate that many secondary learners do not feel engaged in school even when they appear academically successful. Experienced school leaders know that it can be challenging to know how engaged each learner is in any given learning situation. Yet paying attention to individual learner engagement is an important aspect of creating deeper forms of personalization in learning-oriented schools.

Leaders with the mindsets of learning and inquiry understand the importance of being in classrooms and interacting with learners about their learning. This goes far beyond the five-minute 'walk-throughs' that focus on what the teacher is doing. Leaders like Donna who routinely ask individual learners three key questions that are at the core of learner self-regulation, 'What are you learning? How are you going? Where to next in your learning?' are establishing and modelling the importance of learner engagement. These questions are drawn from the work of Timperley (2007), who states:

> Assessment information in feedback is effective when it can answer three questions for the learner: 'Where am I going?' 'How am I going?' and 'Where to next?' Being able to answer these questions promotes self-regulated learning because the learner has an awareness of the learning goals, uses the assessment information to identify the gaps between their skills and knowledge and learning goals and has the confidence to set about closing these gaps.
>
> (p. 184)

These same questions can also open up opportunity for teacher dialogue and reflection. Asking the question, 'Where are you going?' allows teachers to share their vision for their work and for their learners and can provide invaluable insights for leaders.

We have observed significant shifts in schools where the leadership practice is informed by the perspective of Thompson and Wiliam (2007), who have argued that leaders need to pay much more attention to classroom learning:

> A lot of effort and resource, not to mention good intentions, are going into the formal enterprise of education, theoretically focused on teaching and learning. To say the least, the results are disappointing. Learning – at least the learning that is the focus of the formal educational enterprise – does not take place in schools. It takes place in classrooms, as a result of the daily, minute-to-minute interactions that take place between teachers and students and the subjects they study. So it seems logical that if we are going to improve the outcome of the educational enterprise – that is, improve learning – we have to intervene directly in this 'black box' of daily classroom instruction.
>
> (p. 1)

Leaders with a learning and evidence mindset are focusing more attention on learner metacognition and on developing stronger strategies for learning how to learn. These leaders believe that developing self-regulated and lifelong learners is part of the moral purpose of their work. They understand that skills in self-assessment practices are closely connected to self-regulation. Acquiring an assessment repertoire characterized by the nimble and responsive planning and teaching that Dylan Wiliam and his colleagues (2006a, 2006b, 2007) are calling for is an important and challenging change for educators in all roles. Applying inquiry-mindedness to the daily life of classrooms by using thoughtful assessment and learning strategies and then looking carefully for evidence of deeper learning, is an important new competence for learners, teachers and leaders.

Formative assessment demands much more than incorporating a few new strategies into a teacher's existing repertoire. It requires that teachers understand both the core constructs and the spirit of the idea. Jim Popham (2008) provides this definition: 'Formative assessment is a planned process in which assessment-elicited evidence of students' status is used by teachers to adjust their ongoing instructional procedures or by students to adjust their current learning tactics' (p. 112). We are convinced that developing a strong understanding of the research behind formative assessment and then systematically and consciously incorporating regular use of six formative assessment strategies across every aspect of school life is critical in making the shift away from the sorting system and towards deep learning. We have adapted the set of strategies suggested by Wiliam and his colleagues (2006a) to reflect the emphasis on learners and learner engagement and to provide a lens for evidence-minded leaders as they interact with teachers and learners in classrooms:

- Learners are clearly in charge of and own their own learning. Learner voice is valued and actively listening to the views of learners is an ongoing school practice.
- Each learner is clear about and understands the learning intentions of the current area of study. Each student is able to tell someone else in their own words what the learning intentions are and how they connect to life beyond school.
- Each learner has been provided with or has co-developed the criteria for learning success in their area of study. As a result, learners not only have clear criteria for quality, they also know in

which areas they need to improve. They can point to examples of strong and weak work and are able to use these examples to guide their efforts to improve.

- Individual learners are regularly provided with personalized feedback that moves their learning forward. Over time, learners develop confidence in knowing how to improve and are able to self-regulate their own learning.

- Learners are used to responding to questions that generate evidence of learning. Learners understand that 'no hands up' and individual responsibility for thinking are regular parts of learning life. This means that teachers have worked together ahead of time to develop thoughtful questions to use in discussions part way through a learning sequence. Learners are also involved in designing questions that provide evidence of their learning.

- Learners regularly work as learning and teaching resources for each other. They understand and use a range of cognitive strategies and have internalized quality criteria so that they can be productive learning partners with same age, older or younger learners.

The leaders who have worked with their staffs in developing these six strategies have access to significant and 'close to the learner' evidence for their ongoing school change work. As Thompson and Wiliam (2007) note:

It is important to clarify that the vision of formative assessment utilized in these studies involved more than adding 'extra' assessment events to the flow of teaching and learning. In a classroom where assessment is used with the primary function of supporting learning, the divide between instruction and assessment becomes blurred. Everything students do, such as conversing in groups, completing seatwork, answering questions, asking questions, working on projects, handing in homework assignments – even sitting silently and looking confused – is a potential source of information about what they do and do not understand. The teacher who is consciously using assessment to support learning takes in this information, analyses it and makes instructional decisions that address the understandings and misunderstandings that are revealed. In this approach, assessment is no longer understood to be a thing or an event (such as a test or a quiz);

rather, it becomes an ongoing, cyclical process that is woven into the minute-to-minute and day-by-day life of the classroom.

(p. 5)

Shifting the focus from teaching to learners owning their own learning represents a new way of thinking for many teachers who have neither experienced this in their own schooling nor in their teacher preparation programmes. This kind of shift requires a change in teacher mental models. In Chapter 4 we introduced the notion of problem-based or critical inquiry and explored how challenging long-held theories of action requires high levels of trust. From our overview of learning in Chapter 5, we know that people learn from participating in communities of practice. Learning does not happen in isolation; it requires dialogue. The final aspect of the evidence mindset is how leaders can encourage an evidence-seeking mindset that leads to deeper learning-focused action in their schools.

Evidence-informed dialogue and action

Donna had gathered some important evidence about her Year 9 learners and now it was time to move to action. She asked all the Year 9 teachers if they would be willing to look at what she had found out about the learners and help her plan what they might do as a team. When they got together, Donna provided the information she had gathered from their reading assessments, the social engagement survey, attendance and behavioural records, their report cards and her own observations of the learners in class. She also shared some of the insights she had gained from listening to the stories of the young people in the community who had left school. She had been able to video tape some of these interviews and their stories were compelling.

As they talked and reflected on the evidence, plans for action began to emerge. Reading comprehension and social connections were the main focus for their initial efforts. They agreed as a group to look more closely at formative assessment and engagement. Within weeks, the literacy teacher had developed a plan focused on building reading comprehension and funds were allocated to support an immediate intensive intervention. Counselors and local community resources were organized to provide specific anger management programmes for the 'angry young men' and regular group counselling for the 'lost souls'. Female teachers and support staff agreed to form an individual connection with the 'fifteen year olds going on thirty'. They met, they talked, they planned, they challenged each other's beliefs and they learned. At the end of the year, they were jubilant when 39 of the 41 Year 9s successfully made the transition to the next year. Evidence had informed action and built learner confidence and success.

The changes for the learners at Robert Bell would not have happened had Donna not been able to provide a compelling reason for change – and allowed the space for conversation. Teachers needed an opportunity to grapple with the evidence. They needed to look at the assessment data, think about the implications of low reading comprehension and poor social skills and listen to the stories of the learners. They had to find patterns and make meaning before they could decide on what action to take. Timperley and Earl (2008) in their book *Professional Learning Conversations: Challenges in Using Evidence for Improvement* set out to explore how conversations structured to make sense of various forms of evidence can result in real changes in student learning. They acknowledge that 'having evidence and engaging in conversations will not, by themselves improve schooling. Instead the merging process of deep collaboration with evidence and inquiry can create the conditions for generating new knowledge' (p. 2).

In Chapter 4 we provided an overview of problem-based inquiry and emphasized that for challenging conversations truly to occur, deep levels of trust are required. The conversations analysed by Timperley and Earl (2008) led them to conclude that for improvement to occur, showing respect for each other's viewpoints is important, but they add the caution that:

> the purpose is to probe meanings, challenge each others interpretation of the evidence and the reasoning on which the different viewpoints are based. Respect, therefore is as much about challenge as it is about respect, with a key value being respect for the capacity of all involved to learn and improve.
>
> (p. 10)

Donna was able to build on the trusting relationships that she had developed with the staff to create the space where evidence-informed learning conversations led to deeper understanding of the problem and eventually to action. The teachers at Robert Bell were given the opportunity to challenge their existing assumptions about the effectiveness of their programmes and their school in meeting the needs of all their learners and they were able to get beyond denial and rationalization.

In the leaders that we have observed, we have found that the greatest gains for learners come from inquiry-minded leadership in pursuit of intelligent evidence. In Donna's school we saw things shift very productively in a relatively short time period for 40 adolescents. Through thoughtful use of compelling evidence, trusting relationships, and teamwork with her colleagues and her principal, she was able to move quickly to a connected set of actions that made a real difference. We have seen staff in other schools with the same sets of evidence spend months in meetings analysing their data and become demoralized in the process. In other settings, we have seen leaders ignore all the data and make excuses based on the economic and family backgrounds of the learners. It is of little surprise when their low expectations have been met with a corresponding pattern of non-success. In person and in meetings we have heard all the defense mechanisms that MacBeath (2001) found in his study of the responses of 80 principals to evidence – denial, rationalization, introjection and projection. We would add our observations of feelings of depression and despair to his list. We agree with our colleagues, Katz, Earl and Ben Jaafar (2008) that it is all too easy for educators to get caught in what they describe as 'activity traps' – a quick look at the evidence and then on to somewhat unconsidered and unproductive programme 'action'. However, we worry just as much about 'over analysis traps' where educators peer at many pieces of data for a long time in long meetings. In our leadership studies of more than 300 schools over a ten-year period we have seen that the schools that have changed for the better and sustained the changes have looked at the evidence directly in front of them:

- How engaged are our learners?
- How successful are they in the core areas of reading, writing and mathematical problem solving?
- How good is the citizenship of our learners?
- How good is the social, emotional and physical well-being of our students – individually and collectively?
- Who are the learners whose needs are not being met and what are we doing about it?

Evidence-informed cultures

A further question for leaders to consider is how to build the active seeking of reliable research and practice knowledge into the daily life of the school. It might be reasonable to ask how busy leaders can add this to their repertoire and why it matters. A fair-minded observer of educational reform over the past few decades could conclude that in the majority of cases, each reform movement has over-promised and under-delivered. In our own experience we have witnessed 'evidence free', 'data light' or 'consultant driven' reforms promoted extensively, funded excessively and abandoned joyfully when a key sponsor moves on, up or away.

We argue that we can no longer afford this form of school 'improvement'. Thoughtful innovators, practitioners and researchers are now providing, in much more accessible forms, the knowledge base from which school leaders can draw in shaping their own school change efforts. The Iterative Best Evidence Synthesis (BES) Programme[1] is a valuable resource for educators in New Zealand but it is also helpful as a source of contemporary research findings for practitioners in other parts of the world. The goal of this comprehensive synthesis work is to make research findings accessible and useful to educators and to policy-makers. The most recent research summary of what is known about professional learning, prepared by Timperley (2007) and her colleagues at the University of Auckland provides very useful information regarding powerful adult learning strategies.

We have observed many schools where the focus for professional learning has been weak and unfortunately this weak focus has sometimes been sustained for a fairly substantial period of time. We have also observed many schools led by evidence-informed leaders who have used the research knowledge of the connections between intelligence in assessment practices and learner outcomes to transform their school learning strategies in a dramatically positive direction with much better results for learners both in motivation and in learning. Once school leaders, along with teachers and often with student and parent leaders, have made some judgements about where changes are needed, they *then* move to obtaining information that can help them shape their action plans. Our strongest leaders look for some areas of key evidence, form an initial picture and then focus in on acquiring – often quite quickly – the more detailed evidence they need to assess whether their focus and the action plans they are developing are making a difference. This leadership 'cognition in the wild' is making a strong contribution to the well-being of learners in their schools and playing a critical role in transforming school cultures away from sorting and towards deep learning.

Conclusion

In this chapter we have taken a look at how one leader with intense moral purpose was able to build on her own sense of inquiry, the trusting relationships she had built with her staff and her commitment to learning success for all to create momentum for change. The actions that led to improved learning for a group of struggling learners would not have occurred without compelling evidence that focused attention on the problems they were experiencing. Leaders with an evidence mindset understand the need for a range of data sources. They do not disregard external data sources nor do they minimize the importance of teacher judgement. They know that if they are serious about strengthening learning then they need to spend time where learning is happening and for most young people, this is in classrooms or other learning areas designed by teachers. They know that the decisions that teachers make on a minute-by-minute basis have a direct impact on learner engagement and motivation and they are determined to apply a deep understanding and knowledge of formative assessment to make the shift to deeper forms of learning. Finally, they understand that creating time and space for learning conversations is essential.

Creating the conditions where conversations go beyond the surface to challenge assumptions and question practice requires high levels of trust and skill. Designing opportunities for adult learning requires an appreciation for the context and developmental levels of the staff. Reducing the isolation of teachers and creating conditions where adults are learning, growing and stretching themselves as professionals is central to the work of learning-oriented design. In the sixth and final mindset, we will explore ways that leaders are incorporating knowledge of distributed leadership, principles for teacher professional learning and the concept of learning communities as they move their schools to a deeper learning orientation.

Questions for consideration

1   What forms of evidence are you using in your school to determine learner success and learner engagement?
2   How are you sharing these forms of evidence with your parent community?
3   How are you using evidence to plan for action?

4   How deep is the understanding and application of formative assessment in your schools?

5   How close are you to having all learners genuinely own their own learning?

6   What are you doing to ensure that the implementation of formative assessment is informed and not superficial?

7   How are you supporting your school in reaching out to knowledge sources?

8   Evidence-based conversations require a high degree of trust and must involve challenging assumptions. How deep are the conversations at your school?

Note

1   http://www.educationcounts.govt.nz/themes/iterative_bes.

Chapter 7

Learning-oriented design

> It is what leaders *do* in schools and who they are that matter the most.
>
> Alma Harris (2008, p. 39)
> *Distributed Leadership:*
> *Developing Leaders for Tomorrow*

Cathy was using a Book Club strategy to raise deeper questions about literacy practice. Chris, as part of the school's professional learning programme, was involved in Lisa and Blake's inquiry around formative assessment and learner engagement in Mathematics. He hoped that their teamwork would result in increased individual capacity, build Blake's repertoire of instructional strategies and have positive results for all the learners involved. Donna was pulling together a team to focus on the needs of under-supported Year 9 learners. She was taking a hard look at the evidence and mobilizing resources to better meet their needs. Geoff was thinking about the variation in learner motivation and engagement across classrooms and how he could become better equipped to strengthen the learning orientation and knowledge in his school. Alison was determined to improve the quality of teaching, learning and the life chances of learners in her remote community. Karim was passionate about providing his new refugee learners with every opportunity to succeed in their new country. He was working hard with his teachers to make sure they had the skills, knowledge and resources needed to support these learners.

Each of these school leaders was taking action to support teacher learning. Each was responding to the unique context of their school communities. These leaders were constantly thinking about how they could deepen learning in their schools and how they could build the capacity of their teachers through professional inquiry and dialogue.

School leaders focus on learning, set directions, ensure the development of staff, reculture their schools, distribute leadership and respond to the unique contexts in which they work. In other words, school leaders take action. Leadership matters and so do the forms of action that leaders take. It is through the actions that leaders take to design powerful adult learning opportunities that the mindsets of intense moral purpose, trust, learning, evidence and inquiry are collectively made apparent. We call this the mindset of learning-oriented design. This is where leadership thinking hits the learning action road.

Making the shift from sorting to learning is relatively new work for many schools. The examples we provide reflect the efforts of leaders whose schools are in the early stages of making a fundamental shift to a focus on deep learning for all learners. Your school may be much further along the continuum and your challenge may be to maintain or perhaps increase the momentum. We invite you to think about the key ideas that inform the learning-oriented design mindset, to consider where your school is right now and to determine your next leadership steps in designing for deep adult learning.

The notion of design reflects the sophistication and complexity required to create appropriate structures and rhythms for adult learning. We understand that context matters. Some schools have strong and unique cultures that support risk-taking and innovation; other school cultures serve to undermine and discourage initiative. Schools do not exist or operate in isolation from the community, district, local authority, province or state. Reshaping school culture requires understanding the local context, values and history. In designing processes and structures for adult learning, school leaders must pay attention to context and they must have the courage to address aspects of the school culture that inhibit growth and learning. Intense moral purpose drives leadership action.

In thinking about designs for professional learning, we prefer the designs based on 'evidence-informed practice', 'wise action' or 'next practice'. Next practice has been defined as 'practice, which is potentially more powerful than current "good practice", in advance of hard evidence of effectiveness, but informed by research and developed through skilled and informed practitioners' (Learning Futures 2008, p. 5). We are cautious about the use of the term 'best practice' because we have seen too many examples where what has worked relatively well in one school, district or country fails dismally in another. Teachers are justifiably skeptical when a new leader arrives in a school and extols the successes of the best practices 'in my old school'. We have also seen well-intentioned school leaders attempt prematurely to use structural changes to stimulate reform. Too often these attempts failed because school leaders did not invest enough effort in building teacher knowledge, trusting relationships or staff commitment to the proposed reform. We have been impressed by the good judgement of many school leaders with inquiry and evidence-informed mindsets, who have been successful in shifting their schools to a focus on deeper forms of engagement and learning. They have done so by using strategies that fit the culture of their school and the developmental levels of their faculty. They have incorporated knowledge about teacher learning, distributed leadership and learning communities into their leadership work and have made adaptations to suit the challenges of their unique school community. The successful leaders we have observed, including some who are quite early in their careers, are wise as well as current in their understandings about how to shift the culture of the school to a learning orientation.

Recent research on teacher professional learning, particularly as documented in the New Zealand best evidence synthesis[1] work, provides a useful foundation for leaders in their adult development work. Our thinking about learning-oriented design has also been influenced by emerging and increasingly robust evidence about the impact of distributed leadership. Not only does the research on distributed leadership hold promise for sustaining improved learning, we have observed that leaders with the mindsets we describe, naturally and intuitively move to a more distributed form of leadership. The international research on professional learning communities also provides important insights for leaders working to build the collective capacity of teachers and support staff.

We have found that, when leaders are equipped with a knowledge base from both research and practice of what has worked or is working in schools similar to their own, their confidence in their ability to diagnose their context and to initiate wise action increases. Sometimes they 'compose' their own innovations and sometimes they use the 'soundtrack' of an evidence-informed approach; they always bring their own unique imagination and instrumentation to the work.

As we explore what a mindset of learning-oriented design means for leaders, we will draw on several of the principles for teacher learning and development identified by Helen Timperley (2007, 2008) and her colleagues in New Zealand. We will consider the important contributions of the research on distributed leadership and learning communities. Then we will describe and illustrate three evidence-informed strategies to create and support deeper adult learning. We will follow three of our new leaders, Cathy, Chris and Donna as they incorporate principles of teacher learning development into their work.

Teacher learning and development

Resulting from her work with the best evidence synthesis, Timperley (2008) has identified 10 principles that inform teacher professional learning. Four important understandings underlie these principles:

1   Notwithstanding the influence of factors such as socioeconomic status, home and community, student learning is strongly influenced by what and how teachers teach.
2   Teaching is a complex activity. Teachers' moment-by-moment decisions about lesson content and process are shaped by multiple factors, not just the agenda of those who are looking for change. Such factors include teachers' knowledge and their beliefs about what is important to teach, how students learn and how to manage student behaviour and meet external demands.
3   It is important to set up conditions that are responsive to the ways in which teachers learn. A recent overview of the research identified the following as important for encouraging learning: engaging learners' prior conceptions about how the world works; developing deep factual and conceptual knowledge organized into frameworks that facilitate retrieval and application; and promoting meta-cognitive and self-regulatory processes that help learners define goals and then monitor their progress towards them.
4   Professional learning is strongly shaped by the context in which the teacher practices. This is usually the classroom, which, in turn is strongly influenced by the wider school culture and the community and society in which the school is situated. Teachers' daily experiences in their practice context shape their understanding and their understandings shape their experiences. (p. 6)

A close reading of these assumptions underscores the important role that formal school leaders have in creating both the conditions and the context to maximize teacher learning. Timperley (2008) notes that there are three leadership roles that appear crucial to gaining and maintaining the interest of teachers in participating in ongoing learning. These include creating a vision of new possibilities – not through extensive vision-building exercises but rather through every day modeling and actions; providing leadership to the school's adult learning programme through participating and adding expertise; and, by making sure that all the adult learning opportunities are well organized and supported (p. 17).

The findings from Viviane Robinson's (2007) recent analysis of the high impact behaviours of formal leaders complement the professional learning principles and leadership roles summarized in Timperley's work. Robinson identifies five leadership dimensions that have a positive impact on student outcomes:

1   Establishing goals and expectations.
2   Strategic resourcing.
3   Planning, coordinating and evaluating teaching and the curriculum.
4   Ensuring an orderly and supportive environment.
5   Promoting and participating in teacher learning and develop-ment (p. 14).

The fifth dimension is the one most clearly and directly connected to the mindset of learning-oriented design. Robinson's study indicates that promoting and participating in teacher learning and develop-ment has the greatest positive effect on student learning. In her synthesis of international findings, the effect size for this dimension was 0.84.[2] Much more is involved in this dimension than simply providing opportunities for staff development. Gone are the days when the principal might delegate responsibility for teacher learning to a staff committee, make sure that lunch is arranged and disappear to the office during the session. A learning-oriented principal par-ticipates in the professional learning with the staff as the leader, as a co-learner or as both. The behaviour of the leader speaks volumes about the importance of teacher learning, as Robinson (2007) observes:

Leaders' promotion of and participation in teacher professional learning is an indicator of their focus on the quality of teachers and teaching. Such a focus is likely to have payoff for student outcomes given that quality teaching is the biggest system level influence on student achievement.

(p. 16)

Researchers in the USA have also found a strong connection between principal involvement in professional learning and teacher participation and learning. Quint, Akey, Rappaport and Willner (2007) looked at the connections between instructional leadership, teaching quality and student achievement. Their key finding was that greater principal involvement in professional development for teachers is significantly and positively associated with the frequency with which teachers reported receiving professional development (p. 34). They also noted that principals identified by teachers as good instructional leaders organized and attended professional development sessions with teachers and worked with individual teachers and groups of teachers to improve instruction (p. 46). As principals work to transform their schools, strengthening adult learning has to be one of their key priorities and one that cannot be ignored or set aside in the face of competing demands for time and attention.

In emphasizing the important role that principals have in teachers' professional learning, Timperley (2007) acknowledges that this finding comes with such high expectations for formal leaders that it may be unreasonable to expect one person to be able to achieve the desired outcomes alone. Timperley draws on the work of Mary Kay Stein (2003) and her colleagues, who argue that:

Professional development for teachers is not sufficient to change instructional practice, especially across an entire system. Teachers must believe that serious engagement in their own learning is part and parcel of what it means to be a professional and they must expect to be held accountable for continuously improving instructional practice. Similarly, principals must not only be capable of providing professional development for their teachers, but also have the knowledge, skills and strength of character to hold teachers accountable for integrating what they have learned in professional development into their ongoing practice.

(Timperley 2007, p. 192)

She concludes that 'this demanding notion of leadership, associated with the realization that what is being asked may be well-nigh impossible to deliver, has led to the view that effective leadership is and should be distributed' (2007, p. 192). Based on our own school leadership experiences and evidence from our case study schools, we agree that shifting schools to a deeper focus on learning and equitable outcomes requires an expanded team of leaders. This understanding then takes us to a discussion about distributed leadership and the connection with learning-oriented design.

Distributed leadership

We have cited evidence throughout this book about the significance of school leadership and its impact on learning. As we look more deeply at the kind of actions leaders take, it is important to remind ourselves of this significance:

> While we know that within school factors or influences cannot totally offset the forces of deprivation, schools *can make* a difference and *do make* a difference to the life chances of young people, particularly those young people in the poorest communities. Within all schools but particularly in high poverty schools, leadership is a critical component in reversing low expectations and low performance. The quality of leadership has shown to be the most powerful influence on learning outcomes, second only to curriculum and instruction.
>
> (Harris 2008, p. 11)

The distributed leadership model emphasizes the active cultivation and development of leadership activities within all members of the school organization. Central to the concept of distributed leadership is the belief that leadership capability and capacity are not fixed but can be extended and developed. Alma Harris (2008) maintains:

> This means that in schools, as different people seek and are tacitly or openly granted leadership functions, a dynamic pattern of distributed leadership gradually takes over. Over time the leadership needs of the organization will shift and change. These needs are unlikely to be met without fluid, flexible and creative sources of leadership.
>
> (p. 59)

Harris (2008) suggests that one of the reasons that schools are able to move the trajectory of student learning in a more positive direction is because leadership serves as a catalyst for unleashing the potential capacities that already exist in the organization (p. 72). She notes that, although the evidence base is still emerging, what it says about distributed leadership and organizational change is encouraging: 'It highlights that school leadership has a greater influence on schools and students when it is widely distributed' (p. 18).

The 2007 McKinsey Report on high performing systems concludes that the answer to improving systems lies quite clearly in developing better teachers with stronger instructional practices. The report also points toward the need for strong and effective infrastructures within schools that allow teachers to be the best teachers they can be (2007, p. 13).

Leithwood and his colleagues (2007) suggest that the success with which leadership is distributed to teachers depends on the quality of principal initiative. Individual teachers are rarely in a position where they alone can alter the professional learning arrangements or the infrastructures of their school. Changing school structures is most often the responsibility of the formal school leader. Leaders first need to understand the impact of the current school structures and teaching strategies in either promoting or inhibiting improvement in learning for young people. Then, they need to be willing to challenge current practices and, if warranted, change strategies and structures. Changing long-held routines and structures, regardless of how warranted these changes are, can unsettle school norms and cause unrest. Intense moral purpose and a strong focus on putting the needs of learners first will support a principal through these challenges.

Distributed leadership for teacher learning

Leithwood and his colleagues (1999) introduced the phrase 'intellectual stimulation' to the transformational leadership vocabulary. The school leaders we have worked with find this notion helpful, especially as they consider their responsibilities in strengthening and supervising the learning programme of their schools. Understanding the developmental levels of teachers and considering the appropriateness of a range of intellectual stimulations makes sense to them. Eleanor Drago-Seversen (2004) concluded that it was critical for school leaders to connect staff development strategies with the developmental levels of the adults in the school. Drago-Seversen draws on work done in the field of developmental psychology when she points out:

> Much of what is expected and needed from teachers for them to succeed and grow within widely used staff development models demands something more than an increase in their fund of knowledge or skills (i.e., informational learning). It demands changes in the ways they know and understand their experiences (i.e., transformational learning). In other words, the expectations intrinsic to some models may in fact be beyond the developmental capacities of those using them.
>
> (p. 19)

Effective distribution of leadership requires that principals pay attention to the skills and developmental levels of teachers. Principals make determinations about what teachers are capable of doing and who has the potential to make a greater contribution. They also, as Drago-Severson has indicated, need to consider whether the professional learning model being considered for use is the best for the overall developmental level of the staff. Both persistence and flexibility are needed in designing adult learning programmes.

Bruce Joyce and Beverley Showers (2002) have spent their research careers studying ways of improving learner success by identifying the conditions that are required for the kind of teacher learning that translates into better practice. Their studies have led them to emphasize the need for within-school coaching that is personalized and timely. Our observations have indicated that successful school leaders diagnose the cognitive levels and the sophistication of learning and teaching strategies used by individual members of their staff; they think about the staff as a whole; and then they guide the process of selecting an adult learning approach that most closely matches the overall stage of development of the teachers and support staff as well as the learning culture of the school. Then, and this is vital, they demonstrate their commitment to the strategy selected through their active and enthusiastic participation in learning with their staff.

These successful school leaders also consider patterns of distribution as part of their design work. In a recent study Leithwood (2007) and his colleagues extended Gronn's (2002) description of patterns of distributed leadership. These descriptions are useful for school leaders to think about as they engage in adult learning-oriented design. The researchers hypothesized:

> The most effective pattern of distribution would be 'planful alignment' followed in order of effectiveness by 'spontaneous alignment'; 'spontaneous misalignment'; and (least effective) 'anarchic misalignment'.
>
> (Leithwood et al. 2007, p. 54).

The shared values and beliefs that Leithwood identified as likely to be associated with planful alignment include:

1   reflection and dialogue as the basis for good decision-making;
2   trust in the motives of one's leadership colleagues;
3   well-grounded beliefs about the capacities of one's leadership colleagues;
4   commitment to shared whole-organization goals; and
5   cooperation rather than competition as the best way to promote productivity within the organization (p. 41).

In this study of Canadian schools, the researchers found that planful alignment was most likely to happen with the school's highest priority initiatives and that this form of alignment dropped off considerably as the focus when the school was working on lower priority initiatives. They suggested that the most obvious reason for this disparity was the attention and effort of the principal (p. 55). The researchers concluded that the most effective forms of distributed leadership might well depend on the effectiveness of the leader in providing direction, attention, encouragement and support to their teacher leaders. Through these forms of support a more coherent design for adult learning takes shape and becomes an ongoing part of the school culture.

From the research on teacher professional learning and distributed leadership, we understand the importance of the actions that principals take to distribute leadership, co-design adult learning opportunities and build teacher capacity. These actions, through increasing teacher capacity and school coherence around shared priorities, have a positive impact on student learning. Over time, leaders work hard to create communities where ongoing professional learning is simply the 'way it is around here'. The findings from the international research on effective professional learning communities provides another useful perspective on the conditions that lead to deep and ongoing adult learning in schools.

Learning communities

Along with the growing evidence about the impact of distributed leadership on student learning, there is also emerging evidence about the links between professional learning communities and enhanced student outcomes. Stoll (2006) cites the following:

> A *learning enriched* workplace for teachers appears to be related to academic progress (Rosenholtz 1989) and achievement in high school math has been shown to be positively affected by increased learning in a school with a professional learning community (Wiley 2001). Moreover students achieved at increased levels in schools with positive professional communities when teachers in classrooms focused on *authentic pedagogy* (Louis and Marks 1998).
>
> (Stoll 2006, p. 613)

The idea of being part of a learning-enriched school community appeals to many educators. We have concerns in our North American setting about the implication through the widely available 'PLC' workshops that developing a professional learning community is relatively simple work. Our observations suggest that developing a genuine learning community involves a major cultural shift. Halverson (2007) argues that, although the value of professional community in schools is widely recognized, knowledge about how to create and sustain professional communities is not widely understood (p. 50). We agree with Karen Seashore Louis (2006) who suggests that shifting school cultures requires professional community, organizational learning and high degrees of trust. Louis explains that the whole school needs to operate as a learning organization which involves teachers working together to gather information about the needs of their learners, their teaching strategies and their content areas and then discussing, sharing and critiquing new ideas. Organizational learning emphasizes the benefits that can result when teachers and principals regularly work together around the issues of practice that come from examining the information gathered purposefully for staff study. To do this work well calls for the construction of meaningful contexts and conditions under which new routines are practised rather than merely discussed (2006, p. 481) and Louis provides an important caution for leaders designing adult learning:

> Teachers and principals who believe that modest changes such as study groups and team times are a sufficient set of tools to reculture their schools do not really grasp the sea change that is required to deepen trust and create the intellectual ferment that characterizes a learning organization.
>
> (p. 485)

Canadian researchers Larry Sackney and Coral Mitchell (2000) have defined a learning community as 'a group of people who take an active, reflective, collaborative, learning-oriented and growth promoting approach towards the mysteries, problems and perplexities of teaching and learning' (p. 5). They also argue that shifting a culture to one of inquiry and active collaborative reflection from one of isolation and individuality requires a high degree of trust and considerable organizational learning. Lorna Earl and Helen Timperley's (2008) book *Professional Learning Conversations – Challenges in Using Evidence for Improvement* also illustrates the difficult work involved in becoming a deep learning community. Despite a sincere commitment to the importance of professional dialogue, authors from a range of countries found that genuine, ongoing, deep conversations that were productive in creating stronger learning for young people were rare. Again, this finding underscores the complexity of this work and the need for intense persistence by school leaders.

The role of the principal in professional learning communities

Just as with distributed leadership, the role of the principal in creating effective learning communities must be emphasized. The active involvement of the formal leader in each of the characteristics that Stoll (2006) and her colleagues identified as important dimensions of professional learning communities also attests to the challenges in designing a learning organization. Their study suggests that leaders in partnership with staff colleagues need to develop:

1 shared values and vision;
2 collective responsibility for student learning;

3   collaboration focused on learning;
4   reflective professional inquiry;
5   individual and collective professional learning;
6   openness, networks and partnerships;
7   inclusive membership; and
8   mutual trust, respect and support. (p. 614)

Stoll emphasized that creating and sustaining a professional learning community is a major strategic leadership task. The report of the two-year study of 16 case study schools in England ended with this view:

> Across all our schools, messages were consistent; the contributions of the head and senior staff were seen as being crucial, not least in achieving positive working relationships. It was important to engender respect and create a culture where staff felt valued . . . Successful leaders had a clear sense of their own values and vision, as well as the confidence to model good practice.
>
> (p. 619)

Mitchell and Sackney (2006) concluded from their five-year research study that learning communities are characterized by both patterns of distributed leadership and by strong leadership from the principal. They observed that, without the school principal's focused and continued attention, efforts to build a learning community among the staff floundered. By contrast they noted that in schools where principals stayed involved in the process, teaching and learning remained a central focus (p. 631). Halverson (2007) claims that the key behaviours of principals with strong learning communities include:

> Providing meaningful opportunities for teachers to work together on pressing issues of common interest, being physically present in the school, creating networks of conversation among faculty, making resources available to support individual teacher development, building bridges and networks to practice and knowledge outside the local school and fostering a school community in which instruction is viewed as problematic.
>
> (p. 50)

The school leader with a mindset of learning-oriented design understands the power of distributed learning to build capacity and recognizes the importance of creating a professional learning community that is sustained over time. Reculturing the school by developing and deepening adult learning in order to improve student learning is at the heart of learning-oriented design. Leaders help create, coordinate and maintain the organizational routines that will lead to this deeper professional learning. Keeping in mind our earlier comments about the importance of context, culture and the developmental levels of the teachers and support staff, let's examine some of the ways our school leaders are working to strengthen and extend adult learning. Let's also consider how they are working to provide intellectual stimulation in contextually appropriate ways. Let's see how Cathy approached this challenge.

Book club

Cathy's review of student performance in reading had confirmed her beliefs that although most of the learners were good decoders, many of them were struggling with deeper forms of comprehension. Her conversations with teachers and her classroom observations indicated that teacher understanding and application of assessment for learning principles were superficial and inconsistent. She hoped that engaging staff in a book club discussion where they could explore new approaches to reading instruction and formative assessment would be a way to begin deepening professional learning. She understood that if she started with a model for staff development that was too challenging she would likely lose rather than gain ground for learners. Her understandings regarding teacher learning suggested to her that an appropriate start would be with professional readings and invitational applications to practice.

She invited all the members of her staff to meet on a Tuesday morning before school and had a hot breakfast waiting when they arrived. She was pleased (and slightly surprised) when nine of the 16 teachers on staff showed up. They started with a chapter from a book on reading strategies they had previously agreed upon. They decided to meet once a month to discuss what they had read, commit to trying a new strategy and report back on what they had learned in their classrooms. At the monthly full staff meetings, a member of the Book Club provided an update about what they were learning and doing – and made sure there was always an open invitation for others to join. Gradually, the responsibility for leading the discussion at the Book Club shifted as teachers became more confident in leading the discussions. The conversations that started on Tuesday mornings continued in the staff room, the hallways, at the photocopier and in classrooms as teachers increasingly visited each other to see how the new ideas were being applied.

Cathy enlisted the support of a literacy support teacher from another school to be part of the Book Club and to serve as an inquiring and challenging 'friend' to the change work. Debbie's expertise and her ability to ask probing questions helped to extend their thinking and deepen their learning. As the group grew in confidence, they began to bring samples of student work to the meetings and started to look at the impact of their new strategies on learner outcomes. Two of the more confident teachers started to make short video clips of their cross grade learners talking about their use of learning intentions and criteria for success. These video clips provided a rich source for further discussion and planning.

Cathy's efforts to build a learning community and to distribute leadership were informed by the case study of Adams' School in Chicago as described by Richard Halverson (2007) in Jim Spillane and John Diamond's book on *Distributed Leadership in Practice*. At Adams' School, the principal used the Breakfast Club as a pivotal organizational routine to create stronger professional learning. After several years of mixed results with external interventions to improve learning results, the principal and staff at Adams began to revise their views about what constituted quality professional learning development. The principal noted that real improvement started to occur when teachers started talking about their teaching (p. 39). The principal and staff at Adams had learned the hard way about the perils of imposed professional development (p. 40). Their experiences led the staff to develop a series of features into the structure:

- The programme was voluntary – to avoid the stultifying atmosphere of many faculty meetings.
- The substance of the discussions themselves motivated teachers to come to the programme – when valued information was exchanged at the meetings, word got around and people wanted to come.
 - Meetings took place in the mornings, so that teachers would be fresh and ready to entertain new ideas.
 - Readings were kept short so that teachers would have a greater chance of reading them before coming to the session.
- Teachers were able to select the readings and lead the discussions. (p. 40)

The Breakfast Club represented a significant change in the school's approach to professional learning. While the structure was originally designed as a way to open up discussions about instructional research, over time, Halverson (2007) noted that increased participation in the Breakfast Club:

> helped to create some of the key characteristics of professional community at Adams, including the establishment of teacher collaboration and curriculum design as cornerstones of the professional development programme, the de-privatization of practice, the cultivation of in-house expertise among faculty and staff and the creation of a sense of ownership among staff about the instructional program.
>
> (p. 41)

We believe there is much to be learned from the Adams case study. Most leaders understand from their own experience that simply popping articles into staff mailboxes or emailing links for recommended reading are insufficient strategies to foster adult learning. Providing time, space, resources, support, refreshments and a structured routine for sharing relevant readings, new ideas and beliefs and stronger practices, are much more likely to deepen professional learning. Cathy's leadership in making the link between new teacher learning and student outcomes is extremely important. She understood and was able to put into practice what Timperley's synthesis had led her to conclude: 'Professional learning experiences that focus on the links between particular teaching activities and valued student outcomes are associated with positive impact on those outcomes' (2008, p. 7).

She argues that a major determinant of whether or not professional learning activities impact on outcomes for diverse learners is the extent to which those outcomes form the rationale for and ongoing focus of the teachers' engagement in adult learning programmes. We have observed the positive changes that Cathy has created in her school by starting with the Book Club, building trust gradually, encouraging an enhanced inquiry-mindedness, introducing new knowledge and then intensifying the focus on the impact of new reading and assessment strategies on student learning.

Her decision to involve an external challenging friend was also wise. Timperley's work suggests that the engagement of expertise external to the group of participating teachers is necessary because substantive new learning requires teachers to understand new content, learn new skills and think about existing practice in new ways

(2008, p. 16). The involvement of an external person with expertise can also help to counter the norms of politeness and non-challenge that can restrict new learning. Debbie was able to take teachers beyond what they already knew and was able to effectively challenge some of their existing beliefs.

In the Adams case study, the principal made the Breakfast Club invitational and voluntary. Cathy decided to take the same approach and was pleased when a majority of staff did show up. She wondered though about the longer-term wisdom of this voluntary approach. She worked hard to make the Book Club meetings as engaging and as meaningful as possible. She was reassured by the finding from the professional learning research that developing teacher engagement at some point in the adult learning process is more important than initial teacher volunteering (2008, p. 12). Timperley further suggests:

> The research evidence shows that learning important content through engagement in meaningful activities, supported by a rationale for participation that is based on identified student needs, has a greater impact on student outcomes than the circumstances that lead teachers to sign up. These two dimensions determine whether teachers engage in the learning process sufficiently to deepen their knowledge and extend their skills in ways that lead to improved student outcomes.
>
> (p. 13)

By creating the time, space and conditions for meaningful teacher learning, focusing on the connection between new strategies and student outcomes, enlisting the support of an external resource person and participating as a co-learner with her faculty, Cathy is on her way to developing a stronger learning community. She is, however, well aware that she needs to deepen the work by providing more reflective collaboration time during the day and is actively seeking the resources needed to do so. She is also wondering how to involve every teacher over time.

Collective inquiry/assessment cycle

Blake was well aware of student dissatisfaction with his teaching. He knew a great many of his students were not succeeding in his Math classes and although he was concerned, he simply didn't know where to start. He had begun to trust Chris and he agreed to work with Lisa to see what he could do to help his students – and himself. Chris, Lisa and Blake were asking some important questions. How could they work together as a team to improve the learning outcomes for Blake's students – indeed for all of their students? Would the use of formative assessment strategies increase learner engagement and improve Mathematics results? What were the specific learning needs of their students? What knowledge and skills did they need to develop to help their learners? What was Chris's role in promoting and supporting their learning? How would they engage their students in new learning experiences? Would their shared learning and planning lead to improvements in Blake's teaching – and improvements in his students' learning and engagement? Could they build and sustain the trusting relationships needed to make their partnership work?

Powerful questions with big implications. Chris made sure that Lisa and Blake had the resources they needed. Their teaching timetables were adjusted so that they had common planning time and he provided additional release time for them during the day to meet and to observe each other's classes. Together the three of them explored the current research on formative assessment and on learner engagement. A couple of months into the year, as Blake's confidence was beginning to grow, they decided to implement a four-week assessment cycle.

Blake and Lisa started by bringing samples of student work to their planning meetings. They discussed specific areas where their students seemed to be struggling and then decided on strategies they would try. Lisa asked Blake to observe her working with her learners and to give her feedback on the strategies she was trying. Their conversations became more focused and more precise as the year progressed. Other members of the Math department noticed Blake's renewed enthusiasm and started to express curiosity about what Blake, Chris and Lisa were doing.

The kind of collaboration that Judith Warren Little (1990) describes as joint work is critical to genuinely inquiring communities of practice. Collaborative work that improves learning and understanding for young people generally involves constructing an environment in which educator's theories or schemas are shifted through creating cognitive discomfort or disturbance. Bruce King's (2002) work on the impact of professional inquiry on professional learning led him to conclude:

> Collective inquiry also seemed to encourage organizational growth by keeping a community focused, yet dynamic. Coupled with the research on professional community in schools and on

organizational learning, the implication may be that in order to build capacity or to keep it at a high level, in the long run professional development at all schools should entail collective school wide inquiry.

(p. 253)

The team inquiry involving Blake, Lisa and Chris could not be construed as school-wide collective inquiry. Nevertheless it was an important starting place as other teachers witnessed the proactive teamwork to support Blake and his learners and they grew increasingly curious about what this trio was learning. Through his own direct involvement, Chris was not only continuing to build trust, he was also demonstrating his understanding of learning-oriented design. Chris was wise to start with specific and immediate problems of practice. The evidence from the synthesis on teacher learning (Timperley 2008) suggests that effective professional learning opportunities combine grounding the learning in the immediate problems of practice, deepening relevant pedagogical content and assessment knowledge and engaging existing theories of practice on which to base an ongoing inquiry process (p. xxvii). Timperley's work also suggests that through the inquiry process teachers collectively and individually identify important issues, become the drivers for acquiring the knowledge they need to solve them, monitor their impact and adjust practice accordingly (p. xxvii).

These principles of teacher learning have been incorporated into a model of an inquiry and knowledge-building cycle that provides a useful framework for school leaders to consider in their learning design work. The four questions in the boxes are framed from the perspectives of teachers and their leaders because it is they who must answer them: 'But it is also assumed that they will receive support to do so: the research evidence indicates that involving external expertise can be crucial for promoting this kind of inquiry and knowledge-building.' (2008, p. 20)

We think that the questions Blake, Lisa and Chris were asking reflect many of the principles of teacher learning identified by Timperley. We also believe that their decision to implement an assessment cycle will provide them with a routine for their ongoing learning. Their next steps might be to increase the involvement of other teachers and to draw on some additional external expertise much in the way that Cathy was able to rely on Debbie. We have found in our case study schools that when formal leaders and groups

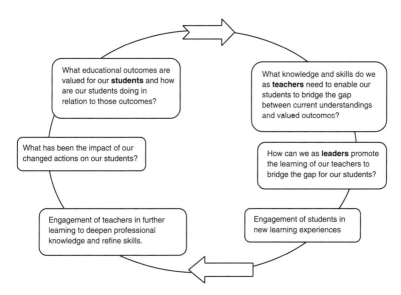

Figure 7.1 Teacher inquiry and knowledge-building cycles to promote valued student outcomes.

of teachers meet regularly to thoughtfully review student work and to plan together based on learner needs, deeper learning occurs. When this process is intelligently facilitated, new adult patterns of genuine collaboration are formed – and through this joint work, positive changes are made to student learning.

Chris's decision to support Blake's development as a teacher and Lisa's growth as a teacher leader through shared inquiry and a regular assessment cycle, makes sense to us. As he builds trust and strengthens relationships with both Blake and Lisa, Chris has become able to provide the kind of intellectual stimulation and support they both need. As a result, Blake is becoming a more confident and effective teacher, Lisa has learned more about leadership and the contribution she can make to the professional learning of her colleagues and, most important, the students have reaped the benefits of deeper learning.

Let's take one more look at Donna and her determination to better meet the needs of her struggling Year 9 learners who were in danger of fading or dropping out. She wondered how she could better engage teachers in considering the learning evidence regarding these learners and how they could work as a team to find and make use of the resources available to them.

Donna knew she needed to do something to help these young people and she knew she could not do it alone. She started by meeting with the learners and asking about their experience in school. She listened carefully to their stories. Then she began sharing their stories and the evidence about their performance and their challenges with a few key teachers, including the literacy support teacher and the counselor. They agreed to form a small inquiry/action team with the initial purpose of becoming better informed about current research on social emotional needs of adolescents and on reading interventions. The team agreed they needed to develop a strategy to change the trajectory of these young people – and to do it before it became too late to salvage their academic year. Donna arranged release time for the group to meet and she made sure the refreshments were plentiful. At first Donna took the lead in identifying useful and relevant resources but quite quickly others began suggesting additional resources – print and people. The group read, talked, thought and planned. Within a fairly short time, they moved to action.

Focused literacy instruction time and deeper social emotional connections with the learners were the two keys to their efforts. The action team developed an intensive six-week literacy intervention designed to provide the learners with improved reading skills and learning strategies to deal with text in content areas. The teachers tapped into community resources to provide focused group counseling based on the social-emotional needs they had identified as important including strategies to deal with anger management and loneliness. The team met regularly to examine student work, to assess the progress of the students and to extend their own learning. At the end of the year, the whole staff decided that the work of improving literacy and social emotional connections was simply too important to reside with this small group and they supported broader involvement. They agreed to make literacy instruction a focus for their professional learning for the next year. They also agreed to listen carefully to the personal stories and experiences of their learners. The action team agreed that they would act as a resource by learning more about adolescent literacy programmes such as the one developed by a Harvard literacy researcher, Catherine Snow, in conjunction with practitioners from the Boston public school district.[3] The team agreed they would come back from their investigations with action plans for staff consideration. They also agreed that they would have some ideas about how to design more professional planning time into the regular school day.

Donna's determination not to let these learners fall through the cracks demonstrates her mindset of intense moral purpose. Her understanding that she needed to provide evidence in a compelling way to get the attention of her colleagues reflects her evidence mindset. Her forming an inquiry team and providing time and resources for them to develop a strategy to deepen their own understanding of the learning needs of these young people and then to put this learning into action, reflects her action-orientation and her understanding of learning oriented design. To do this she had to make effective use of time.

'We need more time.' How often as school and district leaders have we heard these words? The importance of providing adequate time for adult learning cannot be overemphasized. Changing practice in significant ways requires multiple opportunities to learn new information and to understand the implications for practice in a trusting and challenging learning environment. Sometimes, however, the issue is not to create more time but rather to make more productive use of the time that is available. Many adults in a variety of occupations report that they find meetings to be unproductive and a waste of time. Many teachers begrudge the time they have to spend in mandatory school staff meetings where formal leaders communicate the organizational tasks that need to be accomplished. In an age where schools have easy access to a wide range of interactive communication strategies, we continue to find too many faculty meeting agendas preoccupied with organizational detail and mind-numbing routines. In contrast to these wasteful practices, the learning-oriented leaders we have observed often start to shift the culture of their schools by deciding how and when they meet and for what purpose.

Simply providing time for discussion of new strategies, however, is not sufficient. Leaders understand that to support adult learning they need to create the conditions of trust and challenge so that, as Halverson (2007) suggests, they can view teaching and learning matters as problematic. Building in the expectation that teachers, as well as the principal, will try out a strategy over the next few weeks and report back on what they learn creates a sense of mutual accountability. This change in the use of time, combined with trust and challenge, emphasizes the importance of adult learning and provides a starting place for new norms to develop. In conventionally organized schools, structural separations can contribute to functional and emotional separations. Mitchell and Sackney (2006) suggest that bringing people together in a school requires building both different mindsets and different structures (p. 635). In their learning community work, they observed that many principals started by building structures that brought staff members together in planning and decision-making teams connected to learning and curriculum.

In our observations of learning-oriented school leaders, we have seen a range of approaches to structural change. The key is that structures are redesigned to create greater focus on learners and their learning. In schools with traditional curriculum based structures and cultures that are highly resistant to change, some leaders have shifted norms by removing the subject area structures altogether. By creating more inclusive school-wide structures and new leadership roles schools have found fresh sources of energy and creativity.

Conclusion

The research and practice evidence regarding teacher professional learning, distributed leadership and professional learning communities provides leaders with important perspectives in designing for adult learning. School leaders who approach this design challenge with the mindsets of trust, inquiry, intense moral purpose and a focus on learning and evidence understand that developing powerful, context-specific strategies for adult learning is a central feature of their leadership work.

The strategies for adult learning described in this chapter are not intended to represent a comprehensive list for new leaders. Rather our intent is to prompt thinking about the ways in which school leaders approach the complex challenge of extending and deepening adult learning. The manner in which leaders respond to the unique contexts of their schools will have broad variations. We encourage you to consider your own setting and the ways in which applying the knowledge of teacher learning, distributed leadership and professional learning communities might deepen and extend the learning of your support staff and teachers.

In the final chapter, we will consider the importance of learning partnerships and networks of inquiry, challenging friendships and other forms of support for school leaders who are determined to make a difference to student learning. We will explore how leaders are connecting with others across schools, districts and increasingly across countries in their determination to meet the learning needs of every young person. And, we will look at the power of being fully engaged in the 'good work' of leadership.

Questions for consideration

1   A key principle for effective teacher professional learning is to build the adult learning programme around the learning needs of

the students. To what extent is this the norm in your school? Connected with the evidence mindset, how will you determine the learning needs that are most important as a focus for adult professional development in your school? How will you encourage and sustain teacher engagement around these learning needs?

2   School leaders provide intellectual stimulation for teacher learning. Leaders also pay attention to the developmental needs of teachers and the context of the school important. How are you building your own understanding of the culture of the school and the developmental levels of the teachers on your faculty?

3   Your involvement – as a leader or as a co-learner – in the professional learning programme at your school has a significant impact on learner outcomes. What are you doing to demonstrate your commitment to professional learning? What more could you do?

4   Identifying and developing leadership potential in others is a key leadership responsibility. What are you currently doing to build capacity in your faculty? How could you use the evidence from the distributed leadership research to further encourage and support your teacher leaders?

Notes

1   www.minedu.govt.nz/goto/bestevidencesynthesis.
2   As a general guide, an effect size of greater than 0.6 indicates a large and educationally significant impact.
3   http://www.uknow.gse.harvard.edu/spotlight/index.html.

Chapter 8

Connecting mindsets – networked leadership

> In order to introduce, gain support for and sustain change, leaders need a network of strong relationships and clear and effective communication.
> Barbara McCombs and Donna Miller (2009, p. 199)
> *The School Leader's Guide to Learner Centered Education*
>
> Seeing leadership in a new way requires stopping our habitual ways of thinking about leadership and leadership practice.
> Alma Harris (2008, p. 14)
> *Distributed Leadership: Developing Leaders for Tomorrow*
>
> Leadership is about paying attention moment to moment. It is about opening up the mind, the heart and the will. When the mind is opened through a process of appreciative inquiry, judgmental reactions are suspended. When the heart is opening through sensing, emotional reactivity is reduced. When the will is opened to one's higher self, we can let go of old intentions and identities ... The leader's self or capacity to shift his or her inner space is the most important tool.
> Barbara McCombs and Donna Miller (2009, p. 204)
> *The School Leader's Guide to Learner Centered Education*

As Frances greets the staff and students at the beginning of the day, she pays attention to subtleties of behaviour and mood. Which young people are giggling and chatting as they enter the building? Who are the ones who are straggling in alone with their heads down? Does Justin have a smile on his face or does he look discouraged? Has there been an incident at home or on the bus that may need to be discussed before he can settle down to learning? How did Matt make out at his job interview last night? Does Madeline have a lunch today? She reminds herself to drop in on the library later during the morning to ask Anna's advice about some new materials they might be able to order. She remembers to check with Mr Kendel to confirm the date of the community art show because she knows how proud he is of the work his learners will have on display. She has been wondering how she might better engage Ms Sandhu in the discussions underway about oral language development.

After thinking this through with Rudy, her reflective partner, Frances has decided to ask if she might try out a new oral language strategy herself with the kindergarten class as a way of opening up the discussion. Frances is curious about what Ms Sandhu's response will be to her request for feedback on her efforts with the young learners. As she walked through the hall, Frances was interested in viewing the vibrant Science displays using binary opposites and the posted Mathematics work with learner-created images to explain proportion and ratio. The two teachers involved in the imaginative education graduate programme seemed to be gaining confidence in applying these strategies and sharing them with their colleagues. She made a note to drop into their classrooms to find out more about what they were trying and learning. As she went past the office, Frances checked that snacks had been ordered for the teacher and support staff group that was meeting at noon with her to discuss the recent assessment for learning webcast. Walking through the school and chatting with learners, Frances was mentally rehearsing what she would say to the parents she was meeting with later in the day regarding the changes the school was making in reporting procedures.

In schools on the move to becoming learning systems, we have observed the artistic and active way that leaders weave the mindsets together in their daily practice. The mindsets are not discrete or sequential – they are dynamically connected. From a mindsets' perspective, leadership is much more like jazz participation than like conducting a symphony. A leader can start with a learning theme and is open to the different ways the theme can be developed through interaction with others. Some days school leaders are mainly focused on building productive adult relationships, at other times they are weaving the patterns of evidence into a narrative that tells a new story of possibility. Every day they are having individual conversations with students and adults that indicate in action how much they value learning. They are always considering the focus and the design of their professional learning programme, as they understand that this is at the core of ensuring that every learner succeeds. When they get discouraged or tired, they remember why they were drawn to education and to informal or formal leadership in the first place. They appreciate the difference that a shared laugh or a quiet conversation with a young person can make. They find ways of renewing their emotional and physical energy so that they can persevere.

Leaders in schools that are on the move also know they benefit from having a learning partner. Each new leader we work with has the opportunity to plan with a reflective coaching partner for a full school year. These new leaders report that using reflective practice as an ongoing part of their leadership work assists them in thinking about their school directions and actions and in being better listeners in a variety of settings. In the rush of school life where reflective moments are rare, having a colleague who will listen intently and help make sense of emerging patterns can be invaluable.

Leaders with the mindsets are able to bridge two schools of leadership thought. For many years, researchers like Hallinger (2005) and Leithwood and Jantzi (2005) have been writing about the desirability of instructional or transformational forms of school leadership. We have seen that leaders with the mindsets are certainly able to develop a strong focus on learning in ways that reflect much of the instructional leadership perspective. What we have also seen, however, is that when leaders are connected across schools through reflective learning partnerships, there is a greater likelihood that the leaders begin to lead their schools in more transformative ways. Transformation seems more possible when leaders, working in a shared and distributed way, become a collective rather than an individual force.

Once school leaders with the mindsets have connected with one reflective partner and formed an inquiry habit of mind, it seems to be natural for them to want to work with additional colleagues. Frequently we have observed formal and informal leaders form small networks across schools, districts or regions. As these leaders come together to share ideas and resources and to create and mobilize knowledge about learning and assessment practices, greater momentum and support for transformation occurs. This participation in broader networks appears to act as an emotional resource, giving confidence and courage to leaders in continuing to pursue what otherwise can be lonely individual work. In this final chapter, we will reinforce the connections among the mindsets, emphasize the importance of working with a reflective partner and provide a perspective on the way participating in networks of inquiry across schools can help to deepen and sustain the work of individual school leaders determined to make the shift from sorting to learning. We will conclude with some thoughts about the nature of school leadership as genuinely worthwhile work.

Mindset links

As we see from Frances' first few minutes of the day greeting learners and staff while walking through the school, the mindsets are not only linked, in many ways they have become a tacit part of her leadership presence. All the mindsets are necessary and all are important. From our perspective, it is an illusion for a leader to think, 'I will work on trusting relationships first and then, once things are going well, I'll start to work on learning.' Efforts to increase collaboration or to improve school culture in the absence of an intense focus on learning may improve the working conditions for the adults in the school, but we rarely observe these efforts translating into improved learning for young people. Without an inquiry mindset, leaders can slip into living comfortably with the ways things have always been in the school. A leader with an inquiry mindset is always probing for more understanding. Why is this the way things are done around here? How is this decision helping more learners succeed? What is the evidence that this programme is the one we should adopt? What are we doing about the Year 8 learners who are struggling in Mathematics? The mindsets of inquiry, moral purpose and evidence are closely connected. At the same time, the findings are clear that in the absence of trust learning gains will be limited.

We have found that leaders can use the mindsets as a framework for a personal diagnosis of their own strengths as well as identifying areas where they need to grow. School leaders have commented that the mindsets provide them with a useful set of lenses to think about their schools and their work. These leaders have observed that, in their past experience, the professional preparation and in-service support typically available to them has been lacking in the kinds of contemporary thinking about learning, assessment and evidence reflected in the mindsets. Learning-oriented design is a feature of the daily life in the school and the ways in which leaders organize for adult learning also reflects the interdependent nature of the mindsets. In our country our observations of new and experienced leaders have occasionally left us somewhat dismayed by their lack of awareness regarding the genuine strengths of their public education system. Intense moral purpose in our view means not only advocating for the needs of learners in your school; it also means being a strong and informed advocate for education generally and having the confidence to lead discussions about both the strengths and challenges within the system as a whole. It is the synergy in the use of the leadership mindsets that creates the impact for learners.

Reflective partnerships

Frances always looked forward to her scheduled bi-weekly conversations with Rudy. Although they worked in districts miles apart, they had been able to develop a trusting relationship, initially through their face-to-face workshop session and since then through email, telephone and on-line conversations. She looked forward to meeting Rudy at an upcoming self-regulated learning seminar and to seeing him at the meetings of their cross-district school network. She knew that when they moved from conversation into their coaching work that she could rely on him to listen thoughtfully to her and that he would help her to reflect critically on her practice. Frances appreciated that Rudy understood her context, did not impose his own opinions or advice and kept what she talked about entirely confidential. Through her experience working with her partner she had become more adept with different forms of reflective questioning and Frances increasingly found herself applying these same inquiry skills in her work with her colleagues at school.

We have chosen the term 'reflective learning partnership' consciously to convey the notion of reciprocity as described in Jan Robertson's (2008) work on coaching leadership. In this model, although the coach is the facilitator of the learning process, the leader takes responsibility for his or her own learning. Reflective partners do not tell leaders who are being coached how they should lead, but rather assist them to reflect critically on their practice so they can make informed decisions about their leadership (p. 29). Having a trusted learning partner with whom one can talk openly about the challenges of one's work reduces feelings of isolation. When reflection is done well it can also lead to fresh perspectives, new ways of seeing old patterns and a renewed sense of energy and confidence. In the foreword to Robertson's (2008) book, Andy Hargreaves notes:

'Educational leadership is one of the most rewarding and also frustrating jobs there is. The rewards keep leaders going. The frustrations drive them out. What typically tips the balance is whether educational leaders face the challenges together or alone' (p. xi). Both new and experienced leaders have reported that their experience with a learning partnership have made them more able to face challenges, and made their work more rewarding.

The sense of partnership has given them additional energy to think about and apply the mindsets in their drive to shift their schools to a much stronger learning orientation. Our work with graduates interested in leadership has convinced us of the value of including partnership work throughout the programme. Each new formal or informal leader is required to develop an inquiry focused on improving student learning and has the opportunity to work with an experienced leader in a reflective learning partnership during the course of their year long leadership project. Whether or not learning partnerships are part of a formal leadership development programme in your jurisdiction, we believe that every leader benefits from having a colleague on whom they can rely on a regular basis for deep and active listening. From our observations of leaders and their learning partners, as well as from our own experience in a learning partnership, we have seen the importance of providing development sessions for improving skills in active listening and for adopting a set of guidelines to support the coaching relationship. Being clear about the purpose of the reflective partnership and understanding the differences in coaching, mentoring and professional friendship are essential. When the reflective partnership is working at its best, the process between the partners is dynamic and meets the changing needs of, and results in new learning for, each person. This way of working can create a genuinely reciprocal relationship. Once leaders have experienced the power of working with a trusted learning partner, we have observed that there is often a natural next progression to expanding partnerships by creating small networks across schools.

Networks of inquiry

Frances was looking forward to connecting with Rudy and her other colleagues at the next network meeting. Her school was focused on applying formative assessment strategies to build learner confidence and ownership. Their work with cross-grade coaching in reading comprehension was showing very promising results and she was pleased by the number of educators who had been to the school to see their work. The video clips posted on the network website of their cross grade work seemed to have generated a lot of interest. Frances was gratified and encouraged by the strong teacher leadership that was evident in this work and she was feeling cautiously hopeful that if she left the school for a different assignment that the assessment work would be sustained by these powerful teacher leaders.

For the past decade we have been involved with a network of schools interested in exploring formative assessment strategies through a collaborative inquiry approach to professional learning. It now involves 500 K-12 schools from a wide variety of locations working together to explore deepening student learning in citizenship, active health, writing, reading, mathematical problem-solving and, most recently, in improving outcomes for Aboriginal learners. The network has its roots in reflective inquiry and communities of practice. The development of the network approach has been informed by the thinking of Manuel Castells (2000: *The Rise of the Networked Society*), as it has been designed to influence both practice and policy. Reflecting on the successes and challenges of networking experiences in the UK (Networked Learning Communities) and the USA (Bay Area School Reform Consortium and the National Writing Project) has informed the thinking around the design and overall direction of the network.

As part of the evaluation of the networked strategy in the UK, Canadian researchers Steven Katz and Lorna Earl (2008) conducted a study involving a number of the network schools in British Columbia. Their findings have confirmed observations we have made from our direct experience with the schools. Katz and Earl and their colleagues noted that what connects schools to networks (and networks to schools) is, ultimately, individuals (p. 6). We have observed that as relationships and learning partnerships are formed across schools, that informal leaders are drawn to network participation.

Sceptics about networking as a strategy for system transformation are justified in their doubts when the networks they observe lack a clear focus on improving student learning. Katz and Earl identified key features that are present when networks lead to stronger outcomes for learners. One essential feature is that there is a clear purpose expressed through an intense focus in an important area of learning. Another is that collaboration and inquiry need to be combined in a powerful way, so that schools in the network become genuine knowledge-creating communities. They also found that formal leadership creates the conditions for networks to find expression and have an effect. The point we want to stress here is one of encouraging leaders to use these findings in creating new forms of school-to-school collaboration. Our observations suggest that new and experienced school leaders, who are working in settings where collaboration across schools is rare, seriously consider creating ways to form small clusters or networks of schools that share a common purpose of moving their schools much more intentionally to a focus on deep learning.

Recently the international network for educational transformation (iNET) has been creating broader linkages among schools across countries and is providing a platform for an international set of professional learning experiences for both adult and young learners. With the appropriate use of technology even the most geographically isolated schools now have the capacity to be part of a much broader educational community. In our experience with school networks we have found that trust develops across schools as principals and teachers meet, talk, share resources and work together through a cycle of inquiry with a clear focus on student learning. By bringing an evidence mindset to their inquiries and through sharing their findings openly and honestly, we have seen both formal and informal leaders become more confident in taking greater internal responsibility for learning improvement and even for school culture transformation. Reducing isolation within schools and across schools is a leadership imperative and is clearly linked to intense moral purpose. Strong and focused networking strategies benefit learners in schools and can, over time, productively shift assessment and learning practices and policies.

Full engagement

The parent meeting was over and it was almost time to go home. Shifting the reporting system to one much less driven by marks and much more focused on deep and continuous learning was new to many of the families and they had a number of questions. The strong examples of how clear criteria for success shifted the onus from the teacher to the learner, as well as video clips of the feedback from the learners themselves who were becoming much more confident in self and peer assessment, had really helped. Frances appreciated the lead teachers who had walked the parents through the changes and she was proud of their sensitivity and skill. She tidied the papers on her desk and powered down her computer. Before she left the school, she walked into the gym to watch the dance rehearsals and bumped into a group of boys and girls running in from the field after their ultimate Frisbee game. Shouts of 'Good Night Ms S' rang in her ears as she got in her car. Although tired and a little hungry, she felt good about her day and good about her school.

Jim Loehr and Tony Schwartz (2003) have observed that to be fully engaged, leaders must be physically energized, emotionally connected, mentally focused and spiritually aligned with a purpose beyond their immediate self-interest (p. 5). Full engagement means feeling eager to get to work in the morning, equally happy to return home in the evening and capable of setting boundaries between the two. We know how it feels to be fully alive and engaged as school leaders. We both valued our work as school principals and thoroughly enjoy our current work with networks of leaders. We also know that in order to do the kind of challenging, persistent and passionate work of changing a school or a system, working as part of team is essential. When energies are connected, it is easier to overcome the inevitable obstacles. Leaders need to find ways to enjoy the responsibility that comes with their roles in the school. They need to savour the feeling of being fully engaged in work that is complex and filled with ambiguity – without driving themselves to exhaustion. Again, we have seen that intellectual companionship can help leaders avoid this hazard. A reflective partnership and a networked set of colleagues can help school leaders find the complexity enjoyable rather than a source of aggravation.

Our strongest leaders love what they do. Their challenges are easier to overcome because they put learners and learning at the centre of every decision and action. As one experienced leader said to us in a recent interview: 'I really enjoy my work and I think it is because I find it easy to make decisions – because at the core of every decision I ask myself what would be good for the learners in my school.' Lynne has been at her school for ten years, each year building a stronger and more learning-focused culture. Her school has been recognized as one of the strongest value-adding public schools in the province. It is also a school with deep levels of learning in a wide range of areas – citizenship, the arts, fitness, core intellectual understandings and service learning both locally and internationally. Her leadership is an example of the powerful results that come from developing quality and paying attention to equity at the same time. We have observed similar leaders in Germany, Australia,

New Zealand, Slovenia, the UK and the US and have read the case studies of strong leaders in many other non-western and western countries. These leaders are making powerful contributions and are helping shift their schools from sorting to learning.

In their book, *Good Work, When Excellence and Ethics Meet* (2001) Gardner, Csikszentmihalyi and Damon point out that many people in a variety of professions have sought to carry out good work. They suggest that there are important clues as to whether one is involved in productive work: 'Doing good work feels good. Few things in life are as enjoyable as when we concentrate on a difficult task, using all our skills, knowing what has to be done' (2001, p. 3). Those who work in this way are skilled in their professional realms and yet, at the same time:

> Rather than merely following money or fame alone, or choosing the path of least resistance when in conflict, they are thoughtful about their responsibilities and the implications for their world. At best they are concerned to act in a responsible fashion with respect toward their personal goals: their family, friends, peers and colleagues; their mission or sense of calling; the institutions with which they are affiliated; and, lastly, the wider world.
>
> (p. 3)

We do not want to imply that school leadership work is always filled with pleasure; it can be very frustrating and discouraging at times. Yet, time and again, we have observed the rewards of flow bestowed on school leaders who fully engage in activities that reflect their intense moral purpose. The school leaders described in this book are all engaged in educational work that is transformational for their learners, their schools and their communities. Together, they are strong, hopeful and connected. Observing their work has energized us and reinforced our determination to continue developing and supporting new school leaders. We hope that you find this book and the exploration of the school leaders and their mindsets helpful as you continue to work to move your school towards even more positive learning for the adults and young people you serve. Good work is worth doing well together. We believe our collective future will be positively influenced by the quality of the leadership provided by new school leaders with connected and informed mindsets. This is work that matters.

References

Andrews, M. (2000) 'Introduction to narrative and life history' in M. Andrews, S.D. Sclater and C. Squire, (eds) *Lines of narrative: psychosocial perspectives* London: Routledge (pp. 77–80).

Barrett, F. J. and Fry, R. E. (2005) *Appreciative Inquiry: A Positive Approach to Building Cooperative Capacity*. Chagrin Falls, Ohio: Taos Institute Publications.

Begley, P.T. and Johansson, O. (eds) (2003) *The Ethical Dimensions of School Leadership*. Dordrecht, the Netherlands: Kluwer Press.

Bishop, R., Berryman, M., Powell, A. and Teddy, L. (2005) *Te Kotahitanga: Improving the educational achievement of Maori students in mainstream education. Phase 2: Towards a Whole School Approach.* (Progress report and planning document). Wellington, New Zealand: Ministry of Education.

Black, P., Harrison, C., Lee, C., Marshall, B. and Wiliam, D. (2002) *Working inside the black box: Assessment for learning in the classroom.* London: Department of Education and Professional Studies, King's College.

Black, P., Harrison, C., Lee, C., Marshall, B. and Wiliam, D. (2004) *Assessment for Learning: Putting it into Practice*. Berkshire, UK: Open University Press.

Black, P. and Wiliam, D. (1998) *Inside the black box: Raising Standards through Classroom Assessment*. London: School of Education, King's College. See also Phi Delta Kappan, 80(2): 139–48.

Black, P. and Wiliam, D. (2006) 'Developing a theory of formative assessment' in J. Gardner (ed) *Assessment and Learning*. London: Sage pp. 81–100.

Blanden, J., Gregg, P. and Machin, S. 'Intergenerational Mobility in Europe and North America', a report supported by the Sutton Trust, April 1–20, 2005.

Blasé, J. and Blasé, J. (2003) *Breaking the Silence: Overcoming the Problem of Principal Mistreatment of Teachers*. Thousand Oaks, CA: Corwin Press.

Bolam, R., McMahon, A., Stoll, L., Thomas, S., Wallace, M., Hawkey, K.

and Greenwood, A. (2005) *Creating and Sustaining Learning Communities*. DFES Research Report RR637. University of Bristol.

Bransford, J.D., Brown, A.L. and Cocking, R.R. (eds) (1999) *How people learn: Brain, Mind, Experience and School*. Washington, DC: National Academy Press.

Bricker, D. and Greenspon, E. (2002) *Searching for Certainty: Inside the New Canadian Mind Set*. Toronto: Anchor Canada.

Bryk, A. and Schneider, B. (1996) *Social Trust: A Moral Resource for School Improvement*. Chicago: Consortium on Chicago School Research.

Bryk, A. and Schneider, B. (2002) *Trust in Schools: A Core Resource for School Reform*. New York: Russell Sage Foundation.

Bryk, A. and Schneider, B. (2003) Trust in Schools: A Core Resource for School Reform. *Educational Leadership*, 60(6).

Butler, D.L. (1998) 'Metacognition and learning disabilities' in B.Y. Wong (ed) *Learning about Learning Disabilities, Second Edition*. Toronto: Academic Press (pp. 277–307).

Butler, D.L. and Cartier, S.C. 'Multiple Complementary Methods for Understanding Self-Regulated Learning as Situated in Context'. Paper presented at the Annual Meeting of the American Education Research Association, Montreal, QC, April 2005 (pp. 1–40).

Butler, D., Lauscher, H., Jarvis-Selinger, S. and Beckingham, B. (2004) Collaboration and self-regulation in teachers' professional development. *Teaching and Teacher Education*, 20: 435–55.

Butler, D.L., Schnellert, L. and Cartier, S.C. (2005, November) Adolescents Engagement in 'Reading to Learn': Bridging from Assessment to Instruction. BC Educational Leadership Research.

Caldwell, B.J. and Spinks, J. M. (2008) *Raising the Stakes: From Improvement to Transformation in the Reform of Schools*. London: RoutledgeFalmer Press.

Calhoun, E. and Joyce, B. (2005) ' "Inside-Out" and "Outside In": Learning from Past and Present School Improvement Paradigms'. in D. Hopkins (ed) *The Theory and Practice of School Leadership*. Dordrecht, the Netherlands: Springer.

Cartier, S.C., Butler, D.L. and Janoz, M. 'Students' Self Regulation When Learning through Reading in Schools Located Within Disadvantaged Neighborhoods', paper presented at the Annual Meeting of the American Educational Research Association (AERA) held in San Francisco, California from April 6 to 12, 2006.

Castells, M. (2000a) The Rise of the Network Society: Vol. 1. *The Information Age: Economy, Society and Culture* (2nd edn) Oxford, UK: Blackwell Publishing.

Castells, M. (2000b) End of Millennium. Vol. III. *The Information Age: Economy, Society and Culture* (2nd edn) Oxford, UK: Blackwell Publishing.

Castells, M. (2004) The power of identity (2nd edn) Vol.II *The Information Age: Economy, Society and Culture* (2nd edn) Oxford, UK: Blackwell Publishing.

Clandinin, Jean D. and Connelly, F. Michael. (2000) *Narrative Inquiry: Experience and Story in Qualitative Research*. San Francisco: Jossey Bass.

Claxton, G. (1998) *Hare Brain, Tortoise Mind*. London: Fourth Estate.

Claxton, G. (2002) *Building Learning Power*. Bristol, UK: Henleaze House.

Claxton, G. (2004) *Learning to learn: A key goal in a 21ˢᵗ century curriculum.* Qualifications and Curriculum Authority, Department for Education and Skills, UK. Available at http://www.qca.org.uk/downloads/11469_claxton_learning_to_learn.pdf> (accessed 15 September 15 2007).

Cooperrider, D. 2001. *Positive Image, Positive Action: The Affirmative Basis of Organizing*. Available at http://www.stipes.com/aichap2.htm> (accessed 10 July 2007).

Cuban, L. (1995) 'The myth of failed school reform'. *Education Week*. November 6: 41,51.

Daly, A.J. and Chrispeels, J. (2005) 'From Problem to Possibility: Leadership for Implementing and Deepening the Processes of Effective Schools'. *Journal for Effective Schools*, 4(1): x–x.

Darling-Hammond, L., Barron, B., Pearson, P.D., Schoenfeld, A.H., Stage, E.K., Zimmerman, et al. (2008) *Powerful Learning: What We Know About Teaching For Understanding*. San Francisco: Jossey-Bass.

Day, C. and Hadfield, M. (2005) 'Harnessing action research: the power of network learning. Chapter 4 in W. Veugelers and M. J. Ohair (eds) *Network Learning for Educational Change*. Maidenhead, England: Open University Press.

Day, C. and Leithwood, K. (eds) (2007) *Successful principal leadership in times of change: An international perspective*. Dordrecht, the Netherlands: Springer.

Delors, J., Mufti, A., Amagi, A., Carneiron, R., Chung, F., Geremek, B. et al. (1996) *Learning: The Treasure Within*. Report to UNESCO of the International Commission on Education for the Twenty-first Century. Paris: United Nations Educational, Scientific and Cultural Organization.

Drago-Severson, E. (2004) *Helping Teachers Learn: Principal Leadership for Adult Growth and Development*. Thousand Oaks, CA: Corwin Press.

Dweck, C. (2006) *Mindset: The New Psychology of Success*. New York: Random House.

Earl, L. and Timperley, H. (eds) (2008) *Professional Learning Conversations: Challenges in Using Evidence for Improvement*. Dordrecht, the Netherlands: Springer.

Egan, K. (2005) *An imaginative approach to teaching*. San Francisco: Jossey-Bass.

Egan, K. (forthcoming, 2009) *Learning in Depth: A simple proposal that could transform the experience of schooling*. Chicago: Chicago University Press.

Elmore, R.F. (2003) 'A Plea for Strong Practice'. *Educational Leadership*, 62(3): 6–11.

Fredricks, J.A., Blumenfeld, P.C. and Paris, A. (2004) 'School Engagement:

Potential of the Concept, State of the Evidence'. *Review of Educational Research*, 74(1): 59–109.

Fullan, M. (2001) *Leading in a Culture of Change*. San Francisco: Jossey-Bass.

Fullan, M. (2003) *The Moral Imperative of School Leadership*. Thousand Oaks, CA: Corwin Press.

Fullan, M. (2004) *Leadership and Sustainability: Systems Thinkers in Action*. Thousand Oaks, CA: Corwin Press.

Fullan, M. (2006) *Turnaround leadership*. San Francisco: Jossey-Bass.

Fullan, M. (2007) *The New Meaning of Educational Change*, (4th edn). New York: Teachers College Press.

Fullan, M. (2008) *What's Worth Fighting For in the Principalship*. New York: Teachers College Press.

Gardner, Csikszentmihalyi and Damon (2001) *Good Work, When Excellence and Ethics Meet*. New York: Basic Books.

Gardner, H. (2007) *Five Minds for the Future*. Boston: Harvard Business School Press.

Gardner, H. (ed) (2007) *Responsibility at Work: How Leading Professionals Act (or Don't Act) Responsibly*. San Francisco: Jossey-Bass.

Gronn, P. (2002) Distributed leadership. In K.Leithwood and P. Hallinger (eds), *Second international handbook of educational leadership and administration* Dordrecht, the Netherlands: Kluwer (pp. 653–96).

Halbert, J. and Kaser, L. (2006) 'Sustaining deep learning in inquiring communities of practice'. *Education Canada* 46(3): 43–5.

Hallinger, P. (2005) 'Instructional leadership and the school principal: a passing fancy that refuses to fade away'. *Leadership and Policy in Schools*. 4(3): 221–39.

Halverson, R. (2003, October 10) 'Systems of practice: How leaders use artifacts to create professional community in schools'. *Education Policy Analysis Archives*, 11(37), available at http://epass.asu.educ/epaaa/v11n37≥ (accessed 10 July 2008).

Halverson, R. (2007) 'Systems of practice and professional community: the Adams Case' in J. Spillane (ed) *Distributed Leadership in Practice*. New York: Teachers College Press.

Hannon, V. (2007, March) '*Next Practice' in education: a disciplined approach to innovation*. Crown Copyright.

Hargreaves, A. (2002) Emotional Geographies of Teaching. *Teachers College Record*. 103(6): 1056–1080.

Hargreaves, A. and Fink, D. (2006) *Sustainable Leadership*. San Francisco: Jossey-Bass.

Hargreaves, D. (2003) *Education Epidemic*. DEMOS.

Hargreaves, D. (2006) *A New Shape for Schooling?* Specialist Schools and Academies Trust. London.

Hargreaves, D. (2007) *System Redesign*. Specialist Schools and Academies Trust. September 2007. London.

Harris, A. (2008) *Distributed Leadership: Developing Leaders for Tomorrow*. London: Routledge Press.

Heifetz, R. and Linsky, M. (2002) *Leadership on the line*. Boston: Harvard Business School Press.

Hodgkinson, C. (1991) *Educational Leadership: The Moral Art*. New York: State University of New York.

Hoy, W. K. and Tarter, C.J. (2006) 'School mindfulness and faculty trust: Necessary conditions for each other?' *Educational Administration Quarterly*, 42: 236–55.

Hoy, W.K. and Tschannen-Moran, M. (1999) 'Five faces of trust: An empirical confirmation in urban elementary schools'. *Journal of School Leadership*, 9: 184–208.

Hoy, W.K. and Tschannen-Moran, M. (2003) 'The conceptualization and measurement of faculty trust in schools: The omnibus T-Scale'. In W. K. Hoy and C. G. Miskel (eds), *Studies in leading and organizing schools* Greenwich, CT: Information Age Publishing (pp. 181–208).

Hutchins, E.L. (1995) *Cognition in the Wild*. Cambridge, MA: The MIT Press.

James, M. (2007) 'Improving Learning How to Learn: Classrooms, schools and networks'. Chapter 10, in (no editor) *Unlocking transformative practice within and beyond the classroom: Messages for practice and policy*. New York: Routledge (pp. 213–26).

James, M., Black, P., McCormick, R. and Pedder, D. 'Promoting Learning How to Learn through Assessment for Learning'. Chapter 1, in *Unlocking transformative practice within and beyond the classroom: Messages for practice and policy*. New York: Routledge (pp. 3–29).

Joyce, B. and Showers, B. (2002) *Designing Training and Peer Coaching: Our needs for learning*, VA, USA: ASCD.

Joyce, B., Calhoun, E. and Hopkins, D. (1999) *The New Structure of School Improvement: Inquiring Schools and Achieving Students*. Philadelphia, PA: Open University Press.

Kanter, R. M. (2004) *Confidence: How Winning and Losing Streaks Begin and End*. New York: Random House.

Kaser, L. (2008) chapter in J. Slobocan and L. Groarke (eds) *Critical Thinking, Education and Assessment*. London, Ontario: Althouse Press.

Kaser, L. and Halbert, J. (2008) 'A Cross Grade Learner Conversation'. Chapter 5 in L. Earl, and H. Timperley (eds) *Professional Learning Conversations: Challenges in Using Evidence for Improvement*, Springer (pp. 53–67).

Katz, S., Earl, L. and Ben Jaafar, S. (forthcoming) *Networking schools for learning*, Thousand Oaks, CA: Corwin Press.

Katz, S., Ben Jaafar, S., Elgie, S., Foster, L., Halbert, J. and Kaser, L. (2008) Learning networks: The key enablers of successful knowledge communities. *McGill Journal of Education* 43(1): 1–27.

Kellerman, B. (2004) *Bad Leadership: What It Is, How It Happens, Why It Matters*. Boston: Harvard Business School Press.

King, M. B. (2002) 'Professional Development to Promote School-Wide Inquiry'. *Teaching and Teacher Education*. 18(3): 243–57.

Kochanek, J.R. (2005) *Building Trust for Better Schools*. Thousand Oaks, CA: Corwin Press.

Kotter, J.P. (2002) *The Heart of Change: Real-Life Stories of How People Change Their Organizations*. Boston: Harvard Business School Press.

Lasky, S., Schaffer, G. and Hopkins, T. (2008) Chapter 8 in L. Earl and H. Timperley (eds) *Professional Learning Conversations: Challenges in Using Evidence for Improvement*, Springer (pp. 95–107).

Learning Futures: Next Practice in Learning and Teaching. Paul Hamlyn foundation and The Innovation Unit 2008. www.innovation-unit.co.uk.

Leithwood, K. and Jantzi, D. (2005) 'A review of transformational school leadership reasearch 1996–2005'. *Leadership and Policy in Schools*. 4(3): 177–99.

Leithwood, K. and Jantzi, D. *'Linking Leadership to Student Learning: The Contributions of Leader Efficacy'*. Paper presented at the Annual Meeting of the American Educational Research Association, San Francisco, CA, 2006.

Leithwood, K., Jantzi, D. and Steinbach. R. (1999) *Changing Leadership for Changing Times*. Philadelphia, PA: Open University Press.

Leithwood, K., Lewis, K.S. Anderson, S. and Wahlstrom, K. (2004) *How Leadership Influences Student Learning: A Review of Research*. Wallace Foundation.

Leithwood, K. and McElheron-Hopkins, C. (2004) 'Parents' participation in school improvement processes'. Final report of the Parent Participation in School Improvement Processes. *Canadian Education Association*. Available at http://www.cea-ace.ca/media/en/EIC_Final_EN.pdf> (accessed 21 February 2008).

Leithwood, K., Mascall, B., Strauss, T., Sacks, R., Memon, N. and Yashkina, A. (2007) 'Distributing leadership to make schools smarter: Taking the ego out of the system' a *Leadership and Policy in Schools* 6 (1): 37–67.

Lieberman, A. and Miller, L. (2004) *Teacher Leadership*. San Francisco: Jossey-Bass.

Lipman-Blumen, J. (2005) *The Allure of Toxic Leaders: Why We Follow Destructive Bosses and Corrupt Politicians – and How We Can Survive Them*. New York: Oxford University Press.

Little, J.W. (1990) 'Conditions of professional development in secondary schools'. In M.W. McLaughlin, J.E. Talbert and N. Bascia (eds) *The contexts of teaching in secondary schools: Teachers' realities*. New York: Teachers College Press.

Little, J. W. (2005) Nodes and nets: Investigating resources for professional learning in schools and networks. Unpublished paper for NCSL.

Loehr, J. and Schwartz, T. (2003) *The Power of Full Engagement*. New York: Free Press.

Louis, K.S. (2006) 'Changing the culture of schools: professional community, organizational learning and trust'. *Journal of School Leadership* 16 (5): 477–89.

Louis, K.S. (2007) 'Trust and Improvement in Schools'. *Journal of Educational Change.* 8:1–20.

MacBeath, J. 'Exploring the ambiguities of leadership'. Paper presented at the International Congress for School Effectiveness and Improvement. Toronto, Canada, 2001.

McCombs, B. L. (2003) 'A framework for the redesign of K-12 education in the context of current educational reform', *Theory into Practice* 42(2): 329–37.

McCombs, B.L. and Miller, L. (2009) *The School Leader's Guide to Learner-Centered Education: From Complexity to Simplicity*. Thousand Oaks, CA: Corwin Press.

McKinsey and Company (2007) *How the World's Best Performing Systems Come Out on Top*. Available at http://www.mckinsey.com/clientservice/socialsector/resources/pdf/Worlds_School_Systems_Final.pdf≥ (accessed 23 December 2007).

McLaughlin, M. and Mitra, D. (2004) 'The cycle of inquiry as the engine of school reform: lessons from the Bay Area school reform collaborative', a paper from the Center for Research on the Context of Teaching, Stanford University, Stanford, CA.

Mertz, N. and McNeely, S. (1998) 'Women on the Job: A Study of Female High School Principals', *Educational Administration Quarterly*, 34: 196–222.

Mintzberg, H. (2004) *Managers not MBAs: A Hard Look at the Soft Practice of Management and Management Education*. San Francisco, CA: Berrett Koehler Publishers (pp. 292–313).

Mitchell, C. and Sackney, L. (2000) *Profound Improvement: Building Capacity for a Learning Community*. Lisse: Swets and Zeitlinger.

Mitchell, C. and Sackney, L. (2006) 'Building Schools, Building People: The School Principal's Role in Leading a Learning Community'. *Journal of School Leadership.* 16(5): 627–40.

Muijs, D., Harris, A., Chapman, C., Stoll, L. and Russ, J. (2004) 'Improving Schools in Socio-Economically Disadvantaged Areas: A Review of Research Evidence', a paper presented at the Annual Meeting of the American Educational Research Association, San Diego, CA.

OECD (2004) *Learning for Tomorrow's World: First Results from PISA 2003*. Paris: OECD.

Payne, Charles M. (2008) *So Much Reform, So Little Change: The Persistence of Failure in Urban Schools*. Cambridge, MA: Harvard Educational Press.

Popham, W. James (2008) *Transformative Assessment*. Alexandria, VA: ASCD.

Putnam, R.D. (2000) *Bowling Alone: The Collapse and Revival of American Community*. New York: Simon and Schuster.

Quint, J.C., Akey, T., Rappaport, S. and Willner, C.J. (2007) *Instructional Leadership, Teaching Quality and Student Achievement: Suggestive Evidence from Three Urban School Districts*. Accessed from mdrc website (pp. 1–223).

Reina, D.S. and Reina, M.L. (1999) *Trust and Betrayal in the Workplace*. San Francisco, CA: Berrett-Koehler Publishers.

Resnick, L. (1995) 'From aptitude to effort: A new foundation for our schools' *Daedalus*, 124(4): 55–62.

Riley, K. (2004) 'Reforming for democratic schooling: Learning for the future not yearning for the past'. In J. Macbeath and L. Moos (eds), *Democratic learning: The challenge to school effectiveness* London: Routledge Falmer (pp. 52–73).

Robertson, J. (2008) *Coaching Educational Leadership: Building Leadership Capacity through Partnership*. London: Sage. Previously published as Robertson, J. (2005) *Coaching Leadership: Building Educational Leadership Capacity Through Coaching Partnerships*. Wellington: New Zealand Council for Educational Research Press.

Robinson, V. and Lai, M. K. (2006) *Practitioner Research for Educators: A Guide to Improving Classrooms and Schools*. Thousand Oaks, CA: Corwin Press.

Robinson, V. M. J. (2007) *School Leadership and Student Outcomes: Identifying What Works and Why*. Sydney: Australian Council of Educational Leadership *Monograph Series* No. 41. October 1–28.

Sackney, L. and Mitchell, C. 'Communities of Leaders: Developing capacity for a learning community', a paper presented at the Annual Conference of the American Educational Research Association, Seattle, Washington, April 2001.

Schön, D. A. (1983) *The reflective practitioner: How professionals think in action*. New York: Basic Books.

Schön, D.A. (1987) *Educating the Reflective Practitioner*. San Francisco: Jossey-Bass.

Schwartz, D.L., Bransford, J.D. and Sears, D. (2005) *Efficiency and Innovation in Transfer*. Available at http://aaalab.stanford.edu/papers/innovation%20in%20Transfer.pdf> (accessed 10 July 2007).

Sebring, P.B., Allensworth, E., Bryk, A.S., Easton, J.Q. and Luppescu, S. (2006) 'The Essential Supports for School Improvement'. Research Report. September 2006. Consortium on Chicago School Research at the University of Chicago (pp. 1–76).

Senge, P., Kleiner, A., Roberts, C., Ross, R., Roth, G., Smith, B. (1999) *The Dance of Change: The Challenges of Sustaining Momentum in Learning Organizations*. New York: Doubleday/Currency.

Solomon, R.C. and Flores, F. (2001) *Building Trust in Business, Politics, Relationships and Life*. New York: Oxford University Press.

Spillane, J. P. (2004) *Leadership Narratives of Ruination and Redemption*.

Spillane, J. P. (2006) *Distributed Leadership*. San Francisco: Jossey-Bass.

Spillane, J.P., Benz, E.T. and Mandel, E. (2004) 'The Stories Schools Live By: A Preliminary Exploration of Organizational Identity as Story', a paper prepared for presentation at the Annual Meeting of the American Educational Research Association, San Diego, CA.

Spillane, J. P. and Diamond, J. (2007) *Distributed Leadership in Practice*. New York: Teachers College Press.

Spillane, J. P. and Miele, D. (2007) 'Evidence in Practice: A Framing of the Terrain'. *National Society for the Study of Education (NSSE) Yearbook* 106(1).

Spillane, J.P. and Sherer, J. (2004) *A Distributed Perspective on School Leadership: Leadership Practice as Stretched Over People and Place*, a draft paper prepared for presentation at the Annual Meeting of the American Educational Research Association, San Diego, CA.

Starratt, R. (2004) *Ethical Leadership*. San Francisco: Jossey-Bass.

Stein, M. and Nelson, B. (2003) 'Leadership Content Knowledge'. *Educational Evaluation and Policy Analysis*. 25(4): 423–48.

Stiggins, R. (2002) 'Assessment Crisis: The Absence of Assessment FOR Learning'. *Phi Delta Kappan*. 8(10): 758–65.

Stoll, L. (2004) *Leadership Learning: Designing a Connected Strategy*. IARTV Seminar Series No. 135.

Stoll, L. and Fink, D. (1996) *Changing Our Schools*. Chapter 6: The Power of School Culture. London: Open University Press.

Stoll, L., Fink, D. and Earl, L. (2003) *It's About Learning (And It's About Time)* London: Routledge Falmer.

Stoll, L. and Louis, K.S. (2007) *Professional Learning Communities: Divergence, Depth and Dilemmas*. London: Open University Press.

Stoll, L., McMahon, A. and Thomas, S. (2006) 'Identifying and Leading Effective Professional Learning Communities'. *Journal of School Leadership*. 16(5): 611–23.

Thompson, M. and Wiliam, D.Y. (2007) 'Tight but Loose: A Conceptual Framework for Scaling Up School Reforms', a paper presented at the Annual Meeting of the American Educational Research Association (AERA) held in Chicago, Illinois between April 9–13.

Timperley, H. (2008) 'Teacher Professional Learning and Development'. International Academy of Education. International Bureau of Education. Education Practice Series 18, March: 1–23.

Timperley, H. and Robinson, V.M.J. (2001) 'Achieving School Improvement Through Challenging and Changing Teachers' Schema'. *Journal of Educational Change* 2: 281–300.

Timperley, H., Wilson, A., Barrar, H. and Fung, I. (2007) *Teacher Professional Learning and Development: Best Evidence Synthesis Iteration*. New Zealand Ministry of Education.

Townsend, T. (ed) (2007) *The International Handbook of Effectiveness and*

Improvement. Chapter 51. 'School Effectiveness and Improvement in the Twenty First Century: Reframing for the Future' Vol 2, Dordrecht, the Netherlands: Springer (pp. 933–62).

Tschannen-Moran, M. (2004) *Trust Matters: Leadership for Successful Schools.* San Francisco: Jossey-Bass.

Tschannen-Moran, M. and Hoy, W.K. (1998) 'Trust in schools: A conceptual and empirical analysis'. *Journal of Educational Administration*, 36(4): 334–52.

Tschannen-Moran, M. and Hoy, W.K. (2000) 'A multidisciplinary analysis of the nature, meaning and measurement of trust'. *Review of Educational Research*, 71: 547–93.

UNESCO. (2000) The Dakar Framework for Action, Education for All: Meeting our Collective Commitments. World Education Forum, Dakar, Senegal, April 26–28 2000. Paris: UNESCO. Available at http://unesdoc.unesco.org/images/0012/001211/121147e.pdf>.

Vygotsky, L.S. (1978) *Mind in Society: The Development of Higher Psychological Processes.* M. Cole, V. John-Steiner, S. Scibner and E. Souberman (eds) Cambridge, MA: Harvard University Press.

Walker, A. (2006) '*Leader Authenticity in Intercultural School Contexts*'. Paper presented at the Moral Agency Seminar, Victoria BC.

Watkins, C. (2003) *Learning: A Sense Makers Guide.* London: Association of Teachers and Lecturers.

Watkins, C., Carnell, E. and Lodge, C. (2007) *Effective Learning in Classrooms.* London: Paul Chapman Publishing.

Wiliam, D. (2006a) 'Assessment: learning communities can use it to engineer a bridge connecting teaching and learning'. *Journal of Staff Development*, 27(1): 16–20.

Wiliam, D. (2006b) 'Assessment for learning: why, what and how'. *Orbit:* OISE/UT Magazine for Schools, 36(3).

Wiliam, D. (2007) 'Keeping learning on track: Classroom assessment and the regulation of learning' in Second Handbook of Research on Mathematics Teaching and Learning, a project of the National Council of Teachers of Mathematics. F. K. Lester. Greenwich, CT: Information Age Publishing.

Williams, L.B. (2006) 'Honoring All Life'. In R.Cavoukian and S. Olfman (eds) *Child Honoring: How to Turn This World Around.* Westport, CT: Praeger Publishing.

Willms, J.D. (ed) (2002) *Vulnerable Children: Findings from Canada's National Longitudinal Survey of Children and Youth.* Edmonton, Alberta: The University of Alberta Press.

Zimmerman, B.J. (1986) 'Becoming a self-regulated learner: which are the key subprocesses?' *Contemporary Educational Psychology* 11: 307–13.

Index

Page references to Figures and Tables are in *italics*

reflective mindsets 14–15
reflective partnerships 142, 144–5, 148
reflectiveness 98
reform attempts, failure of 118
Reina, D.S. 49
Reina, M.L. 49
relational trust: competence 55–8;
developing 47–58; essential to
learning 44–7; and moral purpose of
school 46; with parents 52; personal
integrity 53–4; personal regard
51–3; respect 49–51
reliability 44
report cards 54
resilience 97
Resnick, Lauren 89
resourcefulness 98
respect 45, 49–51
respectful mind 14
The Rise of the Networked Society (Castells)
146
Riverbank Secondary School 42–3, 55,
56, 58
Robert Bell Secondary School 101–2,
103, 110–11
Robertson, Jan 2, 50, 75, 144
Robinson, Viviane 56, 70, 120–1

Sackney, Larry 53–4, 127, 128, 137
Sakai, Cathy 61–2; and appreciative
inquiry 66; and narrative inquiry 64;
and problem-based inquiry 69; and
refective inquiry 73
Schaffer, Gene 104
Schneider, Barbara 42; on competences
55; on personal regard 52; on
relational trust 45, 48; on respect
49–50; on trust-building 57
Schön, D.A. 74
school identity, developing 23, 24,
36–9
school leadership: in England 18, 24;
and innovations/learning
transformations 17, 20; instructional
or transformational forms 142; with
intense moral purpose 22–41;
learning-focused 81; new, teachers'
attitudes on 118; poor, negative
effects on trust 48–9; role of leader as

intellectual companion to teachers
85; roles of formal/informal leaders
11, 12; work, nature of 36; *see also*
leadership; principals
*The School Leader's Guide to Learner
Centred Education* (McCombs and
Miller) 140
Schwartz, Daniel 4, 16, 17, 80
Schwartz, Tony 148
*Searching for Certainty: the New Canadia
Mindself* (Bricker and Greenspon) 38
Sears, David 4, 16
self-regulated learning: cognitive
strategies 92; and complexity of
learning 92–3; key questions 107;
learning models 91–4, 99; and
learning tasks 92, 93; and
professional learning 93; and self-
assessment practices 108; and
teachers 93
Showers, Beverley 124
So Much Reform So Little Change (Payne)
21
social capital 45, 46–7
social constructivist perspective 84
Solomon, R.C. 44
sorting systems of schooling: and
accountability 104; and industrial
paradigm 14; shift to learning
systems *see* learning systems, shifting
from sorting systems of schooling
Spillane, James 37, 39, 101, 130
staff-student focus groups 55
Starratt, Robert 11, 22, 35–6
Stein, Mary Kay 121
Stoll, L. 126, 127–8
stories 64–5, 95
The Stories Schools Live By (Spillane)
37
strategic thinkers 14
*Successful Principal Leadership in Times of
Change* (Day and Leithwood) 22
sustainability and purpose 39–40
Sutton Trust 32
synthesizing mind 14

teacher education *see* professional
learning
teachers: intellectual stimulation to 77,